VEGAN FOR GOOD

'If it came from a plant, eat it; if it was made in a plant, don't.'
– Michael Pollan

VEGAN for GOOD

DELICIOUSLY SIMPLE PLANT-BASED
RECIPES FOR EVERY DAY

RITA SERANO

Rita is an author, vegan food blogger and recipe developer. She lives between the
Netherlands and France with her husband and daughter, experimenting with new ideas in the
quick, busy city of Amsterdam and enjoying the quiet life tending to her vegetable garden in
the French countryside. Her first book, *Vegan in 7*, was also published by Kyle Books.
Instagram: @ritaserano

PHOTOGRAPHY BY CLARE WINFIELD

K

An Hachette UK Company
www.hachette.co.uk

First published in Great Britain in 2018 by
Kyle Books, an imprint of Kyle Cathie Ltd
Carmelite House
50 Victoria Embankment
London EC4Y 0DZ
www.kylebooks.co.uk

ISBN: 978 0 85783 546 8

Editor: Tara O'Sullivan
Editorial Assistant: Sarah Kyle
Photographer: Clare Winfield*
Food Stylist: Joss Herd
Props Stylist: Linda Berlin
Designer: Georgia Vaux
Production: Emily Noto

* except image on page 9 – Laura Edwards

A Cataloguing in Publication record for this title
is available from the British Library.

Printed and bound in Italy

10 9 8 7 6 5 4 3 2 1

CONTENTS

INTRODUCTION

WHY VEGAN FOR GOOD?

Well, it's simple. More and more people are choosing to eat plants and skip meat and animal products. This choice can be out of love for nature, being against animal cruelty or love for yourself (your body). We are becoming aware of the impact animal agriculture has on our planet. We are starting to realise that if we want a livable planet, we need to change the way we eat. Animals are treated so badly in the meat industry, and it is not necessary at all. You don't need any animal products to stay healthy or alive – that is a myth. Any nutritional benefit found from eating meat can also be found from eating plants. One of the best things we can do is to eat plants. I know from my own experience that eating unprocessed, wholesome plant based food can give you more health, energy and clarity. When I was in my twenties I developed an auto-immune disease and I healed it by switching my diet to eating vegetables, fruits, grains, nuts and seeds. I am in my forties now, and I consider myself very healthy because of my wholesome plant-based diet. I am not switching back, ever.

In my kitchen you will find nutritious, seasonal products. You might think that eating this way is difficult, lacking in taste, expensive and filled with unfamiliar ingredients that are hard to get. In this book I want to show you that you can eat vegan food no matter what. No matter how busy, how tired or uninspired you are, you can stay vegan – for good.

We all lead busy lives and time seems limited. We spend less time in the kitchen compared to the generation before us. But times are changing, people are becoming more interested in homemade food. Even if you don't always have much time to spend making it, you can still enjoy a great tasting dinner. And if you do have time and like to cook, you can make delicious vegan meals for special occasions when friends and family come over. So there are

no excuses – you can make a fantastic dinner, lunch or breakfast for yourself, your family or friends using this book.

It contains four chapters: Weekends, Weekdays, No Time at All and Sweet Celebrations. In Weekends you will find delicious recipes for when you have more time to prepare a lovely meal for family and friends. The weekend also gives you an excellent opportunity to prepare for the week ahead, so this chapter includes some ideas and recipes to get you ready for the week.

In Weekdays, the recipes are all about getting a meal on the table within 30 minutes, plus food on the go and packed lunches. This is for when you come back from work and the kids come home from school, everyone is hungry and you want to have dinner ready quickly.

And what about when you feel that you have genuinely No Time at All? In this chapter, I will show you how to make a delicious and nourishing meal within 15 minutes.

But staying vegan for good is not just about speed and convenience. It's also about treating family and friends and finding foods that are indulgent and delicious. So the last chapter, Sweet Celebrations, will have you whipping up all kinds of delicious treats. Even though this chapter includes cakes, puddings and chocolate, I never use refined sugar such as white or cane sugar. Instead I choose one that is not so disturbing to the blood sugar level, such as coconut sugar or maple syrup. I am always surprised to find refined sugar in all kinds of products, even in those that you wouldn't expect to contain sugar at all, like bread. (If you're interested in the consequences of eating refined sugar, I can recommend watching the documentary *Fed Up* by Stephanie Soechtig.)

So, there you have it – with this book I hope to give you all the tools you need to manage your time, enjoy delicious meals and treats, and ultimately stay vegan for good.

KITCHEN EQUIPMENT

Good, fast and delicious cooking means having good tools in your kitchen. I use these ones daily.

A set of good quality knives is crucial. A good sharp knife is important for all the cutting, slicing and peeling that is done. It's expensive, but it will make your cooking life so much easier. I have a large chef's knife with a blade of about 18cm. I use it for cutting large vegetables like celeriac, pumpkin and cauliflower. I also use two types of smaller knife, both with a blade of around 10cm. One has a normal blade that is perfect for cutting smaller vegetables and fruits, or for when you have to be more precise. The other has a serrated blade, which is ideal for cutting tomatoes and delicate fruits like plums and peaches.

Next to these knives I use a **peeler** to peel vegetables and make ribbons out of carrots, cucumbers etc. I also use a **julienne knife** that turns vegetables into long thin strips, like spaghetti. Cutting your vegetables in different shapes will make your food more visually attractive and will give a different texture to your dishes.

Another cutting tool is a **mandoline**, a manual slicing machine that is ultra sharp and comes with a protector for your fingers. Take care when you use it! The mandoline is perfect for when you want to have super thin slices that are almost transparent. If you are a bit worried for your fingers, a box grater will work instead.

A **microplane** is a tool that I use all the time. It is a fine grater that I use for grating garlic, ginger, nutmeg, cinnamon and citrus zest.

A favourite machine of mine is a **high-speed blender**. It enables me to make super smooth sauces, creams, nut milks, banana ice cream and soups, and it can turn oats into flour. My Vitamix has lasted me for more than a decade now and, although it is a very expensive tool, it is worth the money. It is one of the most used electrical appliances in my kitchen. There are a lot of great high-speed blenders from different brands, so go for the best quality that you can afford.

A **food-processor** with a heavy-duty motor will be very welcome in your Vegan for Good kitchen. They come in different sizes. Choose the size that is big enough for your needs. If you choose one with a strong motor like a Magimix, it will last a lifetime. This machine comes with several attachments and different blades, such as the s-blade, which you can use for chopping, crushing, grinding and mincing. With a food-processor, you can shred and slice vegetables in a jiffy. I can make homemade nut butter in this machine using whatever nuts and seeds I like.

For whipping up aquafaba I have a cheap **electrical whisk** which does the job very well. If you have enough counter space you can also use a more fancy one like a stand mixer.

Another electrical appliance that I regularly use and that I find very practical is a **non-stick pancake maker**, also known as a crêpe maker. I make small American style pancakes with it (see page 59), or my spinach galette (see page 68). I even bake grain or bean burgers on them, too.

When discussing my kitchen utensils I do not want to forget my cookware. I own a **heavy bottom cast-iron pan** that I use for cooking beans, grains, stews and sauces. I also have a **big pan** for making soups, stocks and pasta. My **shallow cast-iron frying pan** and a **good-quality non-stick ceramic pan** both come in very handy for water-frying (when cooking oil-free – see page 10). I have a **wok** for stir-fries and some **small pans** for making sauces or smaller amounts of food.

Other handy utensils for your kitchen include an **ice cream scoop** with a trigger. I use it for making cashew mozzarella (see page 18). The scoop also works great for portioning out muffins, ice cream, cookies, burgers, falafel, etc. I also use a **pestle and mortar** for grinding spices, a **fine strainer** for draining food, a **rubber spatula**, some **wooden spoons**, a **whisk**, **wooden cutting boards**, a set of **measuring** cups, a set of **measuring spoons**, a **pair of kitchen scissors**, a hand **citrus juicer**, empty glass **mason jars** and a **kitchen scale**. These kitchen tools make successful cooking so much easier

A Note On Oven Settings

Most ovens nowadays have multiple functions, like a grill, normal heat and fan forced. Normal heat will be perfect for cooking things like cake, tarts, lasagne and pizza. You can use the fan-forced setting when you want a crispier effect on your food, like vegetable chips or the crispy lentil meatballs on page 33. The temperatures in this book are for normal heat unless fan forced heats are specified.

INGREDIENTS

A well-stocked kitchen is essential when you want to stay Vegan for Good. The main ingredients I stock are fresh vegetables, fruits and herbs, mainly organic and in season.

In my opinion, organic produce is the best choice for your own health, the health of generations to come and the health of the planet. By choosing organic you can contribute to agricultural diversity, reduce pollution and preserve our ecosystem. At the same time, you support (local) farming and avoid genetically engineered food. These are all big advantages, but one of the most important things is that organic food tastes great.

A lot of people will tell you that buying organic food is expensive, but if you buy in season, local produce (for example at a farmers' market), you can save yourself some money. You can avoid buying the much-hyped superfoods as well, because fresh local vegetables and fruits are already superfoods – they have all the nutrients and health benefits you need.

Almost all ingredients in this book are easy to find in food stores or big supermarkets. There maybe a few you haven't heard of, like agar-agar (a natural gelatin made from seaweed), shoyu (the Japanese name for soy sauce) or aquafaba (the cooking liquid of chickpeas or white beans like cannelini). But they will soon become your friends when making delicious plant-based meals. Going to a health food store can be a fun experience, especially if you're used to shopping in a conventional supermarket. You can find new and exciting ingredients that you are not familiar with and that can change your daily 'standard' meals. It changes your viewpoint and it makes cooking fun and a creative process. You start to experiment. If you don't have a certain ingredient used in this book at home, feel free to swap or leave it out. You don't like coriander? Use parsley or mint. You don't have cumin? Get another spice, like coriander seeds or a spice mix. Make a soup, stew or salad more interesting by adding toasted seeds, some nut parmesan (page 26), whole spices or even leftover bread turned into breadcrumbs. Leftovers like pesto, which is easy to keep in your fridge, lift a soup – or you can mash it with avocado and spread on toast, or swirl it into yogurt for a nice dip. The possibilities are endless.

Cooking Without Oil

As you explore this book, you will notice that I don't add oils a lot (like olive or sunflower oil). I eat a diet that is as whole as possible and I believe that oils (however natural they are) are refined products, so I try to avoid them. I choose to get my fats from avocados, nuts, seeds and the oils that naturally occur in vegetables and grains. Instead of using oil, I cook with water, stock or even coconut milk. I use citrus juice, balsamic vinegar or stock to cook my oven dishes. Want some crunch on your food? Then use the fan of the oven, which will dry out the ingredients. Avocado liquified by a blender or mashed makes a great oil substitute. For dressings or sweet baking I use one tablespoon of mashed avocado where you would usually use one tablespoon of oil. Another great oil substitute is fruit purée (such as banana or apple). You can use it in waffles, pancakes or cake. Even nut butters or plant-based yogurt, in moderation, are perfect to use instead of oil. This way of cooking works for me, however it is your choice, so feel free to add oils if you like. If you want to read more about this subject I can highly recommend books written by experts such as Dr. John McDougall (*The Starch Solution*), Dr. Caldwell Esselstyn (*Prevent and Reverse Heart Disease*), Dr. Joel Fuhrman (*Eat to Live*) or T. Colin Campbell (*The China Study*). But still, I don't want to preach, I just want to inspire people to eat more plants and show them that they can be delicious and easy to prepare. Food must not be a religion, everyone should work out the best way of eating for themselves.

WEEKENDS

Weekends are for family and friends. You have more time to prepare a meal than during the week when, for example, the kids are at school or you are working. But at weekends you can really go for it, make a wholesome and delicious meal that takes more preparation or cooking time. I will do my take on favourites such as a mozzarella salad or a plant-based version of a classic meat dish such as a lasagne or steak. You can even invite friends to cook with you to enjoy the process and the dinner afterwards. Because I believe good food is meant to be shared!

Weekends also give you the chance to prepare food that you will be using to speed up your dishes on weekdays or when you have no time at all. So it is at the weekend that I prepare my vegetable stock, cashew soured cream, oven-roasted vegetables and other ingredients I can use later on in the week.

VEGETABLE STOCK

If there is one ingredient that really can be a great base for lots of dishes it must be homemade stock. For the stock I often use vegetables that aren't attractive anymore, but still have lots of flavours. Choose organic products, so you can use them unpeeled, even onion skins. In this recipe I give you a few suggestions for a vegetable stock, but feel free to add more herbs, garlic, parsnips, beetroots, celeriac and tomatoes (you can also use nutritional yeast) when you like. The more veggies in your stock and the more time you give it to simmer, the more flavoursome your stock will become. Only add salt at the very last moment or not at all to keep the stock neutral. I prefer not to use salt at all in my stock as you might end up adding the stock to a dish that already contains salt. Also salt is a very personal thing – especially if you're cooking for kids, you might choose to avoid it altogether and let people salt their own food. One final word of advice: don't add any cruciferous vegetables (the whole cabbage family) to a vegetable stock, they will give it a bad taste and that's a waste of your time and effort.

Makes 1.6–1.8 litres

1 leek, washed and sliced into 3cm pieces
4 carrots, sliced into 3cm pieces
4 celery sticks, sliced into 3cm pieces
2 onions, quartered (leave the skins on if you use organic ones)
1 bay leaf

1 teaspoon dried thyme or a few fresh sprigs
1 teaspoon peppercorns
1 tablespoon mushroom powder (see opposite), optional
salt or umami paste (see opposite)

Add all the ingredients except the salt to a large pan together with 2 litres of water. Put the lid on the pan and set over a high heat. Once the water starts to boil reduce the heat to low and leave it to simmer for 60–75 minutes. Then strain the stock and return it to the pan and season it with salt or umami paste. Store in a container in the fridge up to five days or in the freezer up to three months.

TIP:
I like to freeze some of the stock in ice-cube trays, making it easier for portioning and perfect to use for water-frying, as I have done in different recipes throughout the book.

UMAMI PASTE

Over the last few years, the biggest buzzword in cooking has been umami. It is in fact the Japanese word for 'yummy'. But what is It? It is a savoury taste next to sweet, salty, sour and bitter and it actually refers to the flavour of a glutamate that naturally occurs in meats, fish, dairy, vegetables, mushrooms and seaweed. The taste of umami will give your dishes a hearty, meaty and brothy flavour that leaves you with a satisfied and comforting feeling after eating. It is perfect for people who miss the flavours of meat when switching to a plant-based diet. This paste is for food that could use some extra depth of flavour, such as stocks, curries, sauces, plant-based burgers and stews. I always keep a jar in my fridge to add some extra yumminess to my dishes.

Makes a small jar

2 tablespoons good-quality organic miso paste
2 tablespoons tahini or sesame paste
2 tablespoons mushroom powder (see tip)
2 tablespoons shoyu or tamari sauce

2 tablespoons nutritional yeast
2 tablespoons tomato concentrate
2 garlic cloves, finely chopped

Mix all the ingredients and store in a glass container in the fridge (it keeps for a month).

| TIP:
You can easily make mushroom powder by grinding dried mushrooms, such as porcini or shiitake, in a coffee grinder. Store the powder in the fridge and it will keep for at least two months.

CASHEW SOURED CREAM

This cultured cream is a real basic. The taste is similar to normal soured cream and it is very adaptable. For example, added with other flavourings such as herbs and spices, I use this cream as a base for dressings, and as a topping for soup or porridge. I also use it to make a great mozzarella (see page 18). The fermentation part may scare you a bit, but as long as you use clean tools and hands it always works.

Makes 500ml

200g raw cashews, soaked overnight or soaked for 1-2 hours in hot water

1½ tablespoons natural plant-based yogurt (coconut or soy)
½-1 teaspoon salt (optional)

Drain and rinse the cashews and add them to a high-speed blender. Pour in 180ml water, close the lid and blend until the cashews are very smooth (so no lumps or grains are left). If you need to add a bit more water, start with a tablespoon at a time. However, the mixture should not be too watery. Now add the yogurt and blend briefly.

Pour this mixture into a clean glass container – a mason jar is ideal. The jar should be a bit bigger than the amount of cream you have. Once you've poured in the cream, it must have some room to expand during fermentation.

Cover the jar with a piece of cheesecloth or muslin and secure it with an elastic band or some string. Place the jar on your worktop, out of direct sunlight. Leave to culture for about 6-24 hours. When fermenting, you should see small air pockets appear. This is absolutely normal.

The amount of time it needs depends on the season; on a warm day it will be ready after 6-10 hours, but on a colder day it needs at least 12 hours. The taste should be pleasantly tangy and refreshing.

When done you can mix in up to 1 teaspoon of salt (if using). If you're planning to use this cream to make the mozzarella on page 18, you definitely need the salt. If you want this to be a sweeter cream, leave it out. Stored in the fridge with a lid on the cream keeps for about 4-5 days.

Note: when you are in a hurry you can make a simple cashew soured cream instead of the cultured version above. Simply blend 200g soaked cashews with 180ml water, the juice of ½ lemon and ½-1 teaspoon salt in a high-speed blender until completely smooth. This will also last for 4-5 days.

CASHEW MOZZARELLA

Mozzarella? Yes! You can enjoy this and still be a vegan, because this version of the famous cheese is made from cashew nuts. The recipe is based on one of Myoko Schinner's from her book *The Homemade Vegan Pantry*. The mozzarella is so versatile, it is delicious in the classic Italian *caprese* salad, on a pizza or in a grilled sandwich. You name it, this vegan mozzarella can do everything regular mozzarella can do.

Makes 5 large balls or 16–20 small

1 tablespoon agar agar
4 tablespoons tapioca starch
1 tablespoon nutritional yeast
1 quantity of Cashew Soured Cream – either the
    simple or the cultured version, but ensure you
    included salt (see page 17)

for the brine (optional)
2½ teaspoons good-quality salt
750ml cold water

Pour 200ml water into a pan and set over a low heat. Add the agar agar. Whisk the mixture constantly until small bubbles form and the mixture starts to boil. Reduce the heat to its lowest and close the lid. Leave the water bubbling away for 3 minutes.

Meanwhile, dissolve the tapioca starch in 60ml water and set aside. Mix the nutritional yeast into the cashew soured cream and set aside.

After 3 minutes have passed, remove the lid from the pan with the agar agar and add the cashew mixture while whisking thoroughly. Once mixed, add the dissolved tapioca and keep mixing until the cheese becomes all stretchy; this may take 3–4 minutes. Stir well, otherwise the mixture will burn.

The mozzarella is now done. To finish it, you have two options. You can pour it into a glass mason jar, leave it to cool, then store in the fridge. When you take it out of the jar, you can slice it. It will keep for 4–5 days like this.

Or, for a more traditional mozzarella look, prepare a bowl of ice-cold water (or cold water with ice cubes in it) and an ice-cream scoop. Take a full scoop of the cheese mixture and drop it into the cold water so that a ball forms. A big scoop will give you about 5 balls, a small scoop 16–20. Leave in the water for at least 1 hour. Then make a brine using 750ml fresh water and about 2½ teaspoons of salt. Add the mozzarella to the brine and store in the fridge for 4–5 days.

PEACH AND MOZZARELLA SALAD WITH BLUEBERRY BALSAMIC

This salad is great on a hot summer's day when peaches are at their best and basil is thriving in the sun. The balsamic dressing with the blueberries adds a wonderful fruity and, at the same time, sour note to the juicy sweet peaches and creamy mozzarella. A real summer's delight!

Serves 2 as a lunch or 4 as a side dish

75g rocket, washed

75g baby spinach, washed

1 cucumber, cut into ribbons

3 peaches, not overly ripe, stoned and cut into wedges

300g cashew mozzarella, sliced, or use small whole ones (if you haven't made mozzarella, substitute 2 avocados)

2 tablespoons chopped mint or basil

70g almonds, chopped

for the dressing (makes 250ml)

250g blueberries (defrosted if frozen)

40ml good balsamic vinegar

3 teaspoons maple syrup

1 teaspoon mustard (Dijon if possible)

3 tablespoons almond butter

½ teaspoon each salt and black pepper, or to taste

Start by making the dressing. Add all of the ingredients to a blender and blend until smooth. Taste to check if it needs more salt – the flavour should be a bit tangy to contrast the sweetness of the peaches in the salad. Pour the dressing into a bowl or jar and set aside.

Arrange the leaves, cucumber ribbons, peaches, mozzarella (or avocado) and herbs on a large plate and sprinkle with the chopped almonds. Serve with the dressing on the side and pour it over the salad at the last minute.

ROOT VEGETABLE FRIES WITH HOMEMADE SPICY KETCHUP

Who doesn't like fries? We all do, I guess – they're a real crowd-pleaser. Made with root veg rather than starchy potatoes they become altogether more interesting flavourwise, and these fries are also a healthier option as they use the oven instead of the deep fryer and are served with a batch of homemade ketchup. Now you have fries that contain less fat and a ketchup without any sugar. If you wanted to, you could eat these every day!

Serves 4

1.5kg root vegetables (such as sweet potatoes, celeriac, parsnip, swede, carrots), peeled
salt

for the ketchup
2 red onions, finely diced
2 teaspoons garlic powder
½ cinnamon stick
½ teaspoon allspice
1 teaspoon hot sauce (perhaps the Sambal, see page 90) or chilli flakes
1½ tablespoons mushroom powder (see Tip, page 15)
1 teaspoon smoked paprika
500ml tomato sauce (see Tip, page 30) or a good-quality shopbought one
3–4 teaspoons maple syrup
1 tablespoon (white) balsamic vinegar
shoyu sauce or sea salt, to taste

Preheat the oven on 220°C fan/240°C/gas mark 9 and line two baking trays with baking paper.

Bring a large pan of water to the boil. Cut the root vegetables into fries, roughly the same shape. When the water boils add the vegetables and blanch for 2–3 minutes. Drain and leave in a colander to remove as much moisture as you can. Arrange the fries in a single layer on the lined trays. Sprinkle with salt to taste. Bake the fries for 25–30 minutes, turning them from time to time until golden and crisp.

Meanwhile make the ketchup. Water-fry the red onions in a large pan using either a little water or stock until translucent. Then add the garlic powder, cinnamon, allspice, hot sauce, mushroom powder and smoked paprika. Stir to coat the onions with the spices and cook them for a further minute. If needed, add another splash of water or stock to prevent burning. Then add the tomato sauce, maple syrup, balsamic vinegar and shoyu or salt to taste. Bring to the boil then reduce the heat and leave the ketchup to simmer for 10–15 minutes. Leave to cool. (Of course, the ketchup can be made in advance. It will keep for 10–14 days in the fridge.)

When the fries are crispy and golden brown serve them with the spicy ketchup.

TWO SAVOURY TOPPINGS

How do you make a simple dish more interesting? Simply add a bit of crunch and concentrated taste. I often make a big jar of crunchy toppings at the weekend, so when I am in a hurry making a meal such as a soup, salad or stew, I can add a bit of these toppings to make an ordinary common dish stand out.

ALMOND AND SESAME TOPPING – Makes about 200g

2 teaspoons umami paste (see page 15) or soy sauce
2 teaspoons maple syrup
1 teaspoon rice vinegar or balsamic vinegar
good pinch of chilli

2 teaspoons aquafaba (chickpea cooking liquid, see page 135)
100g chopped almonds
50g white sesame seeds
50g black sesame seeds

Preheat the oven to 180°C/gas mark 4 and line a baking tray with baking paper.

Mix the umami paste, maple syrup, rice vinegar or balsamic vinegar, chilli and aquafaba in a small bowl. Mix the almonds and seeds in another bowl, then mix with the liquid until all ingredients are fully coated.

Spread the nuts and seeds on the lined tray and bake for 6 minutes in the middle of the oven, then turn the nuts and seeds and bake for a further 6–8 minutes. Keep a close eye on them and turn again if needed – you don't want them to burn. The almonds should be golden brown and the mixture dry in the centre. Remove the mixture from the oven and leave to cool before storing it in a glass jar with a tight-fitting lid. It will keep for 2–3 weeks.

MAPLE MUSTARD TOPPING – Makes about 200g

1½ teaspoons Dijon mustard
2 teaspoons maple syrup
1 teaspoon balsamic vinegar
2 teaspoons aquafaba (chickpea cooking
   liquid, see page 135)
3 tablespoons nutritional yeast

1 teaspoon dried thyme
½ teaspoon salt
50g rolled oats
50g pine nuts
50g pumpkin seeds
50g sunflower seeds

Preheat the oven to 180°C/gas mark 4 and line a baking tray with baking paper. Mix the Dijon mustard, maple syrup, balsamic vinegar, aquafaba, nutritional yeast, thyme and salt in a small bowl. In another bowl combine the oats, pine nuts, pumpkin seeds and sunflower seeds. Now add the wet mixture to the dry mixture. Stir until all the ingredients are fully coated.

Spread the mixture on the lined tray and bake for 6–8 minutes in the middle of the oven, then turn the nuts and seeds and bake for a further 6–8 minutes until they are golden brown, and the mixture is dry in the centre. Remove the mixture from the oven and leave to cool before storing it in a glass jar with a tight-fitting lid. It will keep for 2–3 weeks.

NUT PARMESAN

In the past, I followed a raw diet; I did this for seven years. During this time I learned new techniques to prepare ingredients and fun ways to swap animal-based food for plant-based food. One of the first (and probably one of the easiest) substitutions I learned was to make nut Parmesan. The secret ingredient to make it 'cheesy' is nutritional yeast. This yellow yeast is flaky (like grated Parmesan) and can be found in health food stores. The nut Parmesan can (of course) be used on pasta, but it also tastes great in soups and salads, and on roasted vegetables and (plant-based) burgers. Make twice as much if you want, because it will disappear quick!

Makes about 100g

50g pine nuts

50g raw, unsalted cashews

1 tablespoon nutritional yeast

½ teaspoon onion powder

½ teaspoon garlic powder

Simply blend all the ingredients in a high-speed blender until a grated Parmesan-like structure appears. This will keep for a week in the fridge.

> **TIP:**
> Add nuts and seeds to change the taste of this Parmesan according to your liking. Think of walnuts, blanced almonds, sunflower seeds, blanched hazelnuts or macadamia. As long as the nuts and seeds are light in colour, it will be the same colour as traditional Parmesan. If you like a stronger taste, you can add more nutritional yeast and salt. The best way to store nut Parmesan is in a glass jar in a cool, dry place.

FLATBREAD

From a few simple ingredients – flour, water and salt – you can quickly make flatbreads. Known variously as tortilla, chapati, injeera, roti and matzo, flatbreads are eaten all around the world. They make a great accompaniment or a base for all kinds of dishes and are prepared quickly because they don't involve yeast. This basic recipe is simple to learn and fun to make. Don't hold back: make as many as you want and freeze them until needed.

Makes 8 large flatbreads

450g wholegrain spelt flour (you can use
    sprouted or even a gluten-free mix)
1 teaspoon good-quality salt

2½ teaspoons baking powder
240ml hot water

Mix the flour, salt and baking powder in a large bowl. Add the hot water and start mixing it in using a fork first. Then use your hands until a ball forms. Continue to knead for 3–4 minutes until smooth, either in the bowl or on a clean work surface dusted with some flour. Return the dough to the bowl, cover it with a clean, damp towel and leave it to rest for about 15–30 minutes.

Divide your dough into eight equally sized balls. Place a large frying pan over a medium to high heat. Flatten a ball a little with your hands then roll out on a clean, lightly floured surface to a diameter of about 20cm. You may need to flour your flatbread lightly, too, so that it doesn't stick to either the rolling pin or the surface.

Once the pan is hot, place the first flatbread in the pan and let it cook until it starts to puff up a bit – this will take about 1–2 minutes. Then flip over the flatbread and cook the other side for about a minute. When ready, transfer to a plate under a clean, damp towel. Repeat until all the flatbreads are cooked.

Serve immediately or store the flatbreads in the freezer – I layer them with baking paper, so they can be separated easily.

BLACK BEAN QUESADILLA WITH KIWI AND JALAPEÑO SALSA VERDE

On weekdays my daughter is at school during lunch hours and I am working behind a computer screen or testing a new recipe, so lunch ends up being a quickly made sandwich, a few bites of what I am testing or leftovers from the day before. On weekends we have time to sit together and eat a proper lunch with the whole family. This quesadilla is not a fast food snack, it's a real, wholesome cooked meal that can be shared with loved ones.

Serves 2 for dinner or 4 as a light lunch

2 flatbreads (see page 27)

for the filling
1 red onion, chopped
120ml stock or water, plus extra for frying
3 garlic cloves, finely chopped
1½ tablespoons tomato purée
1½ teaspoons dried oregano
1½ teaspoons ground cumin
1½ teaspoons chipotle powder (or 1 teaspoon smoked hot paprika)
½ teaspoon ground cinnamon
½ teaspoon ground star anise
480g (drained weight) black beans from two

440g jars or cans)
½ teaspoon salt (or more to taste)
2 small ripe avocados, mashed

for the salsa verde
5 kiwi fruit, not overly ripe, peeled and quartered
3 spring onions, finely sliced
1 fresh jalapeño pepper, deseeded and finely chopped (for less heat use ½) or 2 tablespoons jalapeño slices from a jar, chopped
bunch of fresh coriander, washed and chopped
juice of 1 lime
½ teaspoon salt

Start by making the bean filling. Heat a non-stick frying pan until hot, add the onion and allow to caramelise but not burn: watch it carefully. Once the pieces turn a little brown, add a splash of water or tasty stock. Keep stirring and add some extra water or stock when needed. After 4–5 minutes add the garlic, tomato purée, herbs and spices. Mix to coat the onion evenly. Then add the stock or water, drained black beans and salt. Cook for about 8 minutes, mashing the black beans just a little so that the mixture gets creamier, but leave some texture. Remove the pan from the heat.

Make the salsa by chopping all the ingredients (except the lime juice) by hand or pulse chop

them in a food processor. Now add the lime juice and salt. Taste and, if needed, add more.

Place one flatbread on a clean chopping board and spread all the bean mixture evenly over the bread. Now spread the mashed avocado over the bean mixture. Top with the second flatbread.

Heat a dry frying pan (I like to use a cast-iron one) and toast the quesadilla on each side for a few minutes. To flip the quesadilla more easily, invert the pan over a large plate and then slide the quesadilla back into the pan. Cut the quesadilla into 6–8 pieces and spoon over the kiwi salsa.

SLOW-ROASTED CHERRY TOMATOES

In late summer, when tomatoes are at their very best, I always end up buying way too many so, to preserve them, I slow-roast tomatoes in the oven. Slow-roasting intensifies the flavours. For a real flavour hit, add some to salads, bowls, lunches or pasta. Otherwise, blend them into an incredibly flavoured tomato sauce, which can also be used in other dishes, like homemade ketchup (see page 22) or simply spread the sauce on a flatbread to make a super-quick pizza (see page 62).

Makes around 500–750g

1kg cherry tomatoes, halved
2 tablespoons (white) balsamic vinegar
1-2 garlic cloves, chopped

¾ teaspoon good-quality salt (preferably smoked)
a few sprigs of thyme (optional)

Preheat the oven to 130°C/gas mark ½. Mix the cherry tomatoes, balsamic vinegar, garlic, salt and herbs in a bowl. Spread the mixture on a baking tray and bake in the oven for 3–4 hours.

When the tomatoes are ready they will be soft and have released their juices. Remove from the oven, allow to cool and store in the fridge. They will keep for 4–5 days.

TIP:
Blend the tomatoes to make 500ml of incredibly delicious tomato sauce that can be used in pasta dishes, stews and curries or as a base for a pizza.

PERFECTLY COOKED LENTILS

Puy, beluga or plain brown lentils are one of my favourite ingredients. They don't require pre-soaking, unlike larger pulses. They keep their shape really well and they can be added to lots of dishes and transformed into entirely new recipes. I usually make a large batch at the weekend, so I can grab them easily out of the fridge. Cooking lentils yourself saves you money (buying individual tins or jars is much more expensive), avoids extra packaging (less waste) and they are (of course) very delicious. The key to cooking lentils is thorough rinsing. Boil them with aromatics to get even more taste. However do not add any salt while boiling, because salt slows down the whole cooking process, which results in tougher skins. Add salt *after* the lentils are cooked.

Makes about 1–1.2kg

500g Puy, beluga or brown lentils
1 head of garlic, sliced in half horizontally
1 onion, halved
1 teaspoon fennel seeds

1 bay leaf, cracked
1 teaspoon dried thyme (optional)
1 teaspoon chilli flakes (optional)

Wash the lentils by thoroughly rinsing them in a colander with cold water. Transfer them to a large cooking pot with 1.2 litres of cold water and the garlic, onion, fennel seeds, bay leaf and thyme and chilli (if using).

Bring to the boil over a medium–high heat, scraping off and discarding any foam that appears on the surface (this can contain impurities that you did not catch with the rinsing).

Once the water boils, reduce the heat to low and simmer for 20 minutes. After this time the lentils should be cooked but still a bit firm when you

bite into them – 'al dente', as the Italians say. If you prefer them softer, add 3–5 minutes to the cooking time, but no longer, otherwise the lentils will start to fall apart.

Turn off the heat and add salt to taste. Leave to cool, then store in the fridge or in your freezer. If you decide to freeze the lentils, I'd suggest freezing them in four batches of 250–300g as these are more suitable amounts for smaller households and will be easier to defrost.

> **TIP:**
> For extra depth of flavour add 1 or 2 tablespoons of umami paste (see page 15) mixed with
> 1 tablespoon of water to the cooked lentils (instead of salt).

LENTIL AND MUSHROOM 'MEATBALLS' WITH TOMATO SAUCE

One might think of meatballs in tomato sauce as a typical traditional Italian dish, but it is actually more American Italian. In the early twentieth century meat was expensive and many families in Italy were poor. They were used to eating pasta and tomato sauce with only a bit of meat or none at all. In search of a better life many Italians migrated to America. In time, as their standards of living improved, the 'bits of meat' became 'meatballs'. This shows how dishes can be transformed over time. I wanted to transform this dish even further and so have changed the 'meatballs' into mushroom and lentil balls.

Serves 4 (makes about 20 'meatballs')

1 medium onion, chopped

250g button mushrooms (or other variety), chopped mushrooms

60ml stock or water, plus extra for frying

2 garlic cloves, chopped

2 teaspoons dried oregano

½ teaspoon ground fennel seeds (you can easily grind the seeds using a mortar and pestle)

½ teaspoon chilli powder

1 rounded teaspoon tomato purée

240g (drained weight) cooked green or Beluga lentils (see page opposite), or from a 400g jar/

can, drained and roughly mashed with a fork

150g cooked bulgur wheat (or quinoa or rice)

50g rolled oats

10g nutritional yeast (optional)

500ml homemade tomato sauce (see page 30)

small bunch of fresh basil (optional), leaves torn

salt and freshly ground black pepper

300g wholegrain pasta of choice, to serve

Preheat the oven to 200°C fan/220°C/gas mark 7 and line a baking tray with baking paper.

Heat a non-stick frying pan until hot and add the onions and mushrooms with a splash of water or stock. Allow them to start to caramelise and, if needed, add some extra water or stock (a splash at a time). Once the onions and mushrooms have softened, add the garlic, herbs, spices and tomato purée. Now add about 60ml of water or stock and cook for 4–5 minutes.

Remove the pan from the heat and tip the mixture into a large bowl. Add the lentils, cooked grain, rolled oats and nutritional yeast. Mix

thoroughly and add salt and black pepper to taste. You can also mix this in a food-processor by pulse chopping it a couple of times. Make small balls of this mixture, either using a small ice cream scoop or by taking about 1½ tablespoonfuls to roll with clean, moist hands. Lay each ball on the lined tray and continue to do so until all the mixture is gone. Cook the balls in the oven for 20 minutes – you want them a little crisp on the outside and moist inside.

Meanwhile, warm the tomato sauce and add most of the torn basil to it. Keep some of the basil aside for later. Leave the sauce to simmer.

continued ——— ———→

⟶ Cook the pasta according to the packet instructions. Once cooked, drain the pasta in a colander, reserving some of the cooking liquid. Return the pasta to the pan and add a couple of tablespoons of the cooking liquid. This prevents the pasta from sticking together and you won't have to add any oils. Add the balls to the sauce and serve with the pasta and freshly torn basil on top.

TIP:

These 'faux' meatballs have an Italian seasoning, but they can easily be adapted to other flavours as well. Use 1 teaspoon of ground cumin, 1 teaspoon of oregano and 1 teaspoon of paprika and serve it with the kiwi salsa from page 28 for a Mexican-inspired dish. Add 1–2 tablespoons of your favourite curry paste and serve the meatballs with cooked or stir-fried noodles to make the dish more Asian-themed. For a North African taste, add 1 teaspoon of ground cumin, 1 teaspoon of ground coriander, ½ teaspoon of cinnamon and 1–2 teaspoons of harissa paste.

WHOLE ROASTED CELERIAC

I like to roast my vegetables whole. The skin acts as a natural alternative to foil and retains all the moisture. This way of cooking is fuss free, has no waste (e.g. aluminium foil) and really makes the flavour of the vegetable stand out. Use the roasted celeriac in soups, stews, salad or as a celeriac steak (see page 38).

Makes 8 slices

1 whole celeriac, well washed and, if needed, scrubbed

Preheat the oven to 200°C/gas mark 6. Place the whole celeriac onto a baking dish and cook for 1½–2 hours. It is ready when you can easily pierce it through with a knife. Remove the celeriac from the oven and allow to cool.

When the celeriac is cool enough to handle, cut off the skin using a sharp knife. Now cut the celeriac horizontally into eight slices about 2cm thick. Store the slices in the fridge for use later in the week or serve them straight away as celeriac steaks (see page 38).

GRILLED CELERIAC STEAKS WITH CASHEW TARTARE

It's easy to make 'steaks' from a whole roasted celeriac. You can grill them on a griddle pan or, in summer, put them on the barbecue.

Serves 4

8 celeriac steaks (see previous recipe)
green salad and cooked grains or potatoes,
  to serve

for the tartare
500ml Cashew Soured Cream (see page 17)
6 tablespoons chopped sour gherkins

 (ensure they are sugar-free)
6 tablespoons chopped capers
30g flat-leaf parsley, chopped
1 tablespoon Dijon mustard
juice of ½ lemon
salt and freshly ground black pepper

Heat a cast-iron griddle pan (or a panini maker). Ensure you have the heat high. Once hot, add as many steaks as will fit, allowing enough room to flip them. You may have to do this in batches. Cook the steak on one side for about 2–3 minutes until a grill pattern forms. Flip them over and cook the steaks for the same time on the other side. Remove the steaks from the pan and put them between two plates in the oven on a low temperature to keep warm while you cook the remaining steaks and get the sauce ready.

Meanwhile make the tartare sauce by mixing all the ingredients and adding salt and pepper to taste. Serve the steaks with the sauce on the side, along with some green salad and cooked grains or potatoes.

SAVOURY BEETROOT MUFFINS

Cake salé ('salty cake') is not part of Dutch cuisine. I was introduced to it by a French friend and I really wanted to make my own savoury cake. The key feature of the cake is that it's light in texture. Normal cakes include eggs to accomplish this, but here aquafaba gives these hearty muffins a nice airy touch. Beetroot is naturally a bit sweet so these savoury muffins benefit from the contrast provided by the salty olives. All in all, I think I've succeeded in my mission to make a vegan *cake salé*.

Makes 10-12 muffins

70g pumpkin seeds

1½ raw medium red beetroots, peeled

6 tablespoons aquafaba (chickpea cooking liquid, see page 135), chilled

200g wholegrain spelt flour

50g oat flakes

2 teaspoons baking powder

1 teaspoon bicarbonate of soda

2 tablespoons nutritional yeast (optional)

1 teaspoon each salt and ground black pepper

300ml natural plant-based yogurt

small bunch of chives, finely chopped

2 tablespoons freshly chopped thyme

70g pitted black olives, chopped

Preheat the oven to 200°C/gas mark 6. Heat a cast-iron or non-stick pan and dry-roast the pumpkin seeds until they start to pop. Set aside.

Finely grate the beetroot using a food-processor, mandoline or box grater. Set aside.

Whip the aquafaba in a clean bowl using hand-held electric beaters or a stand mixer until stiff white peaks form.

In another bowl mix the flour, oat flakes, baking powder, bicarbonate of soda, nutritional yeast (if using), salt and pepper.

In a blender mix together the yogurt and beetroot until combined. Add this to the flour mixture, along with the herbs, chopped olives and whipped aquafaba. Mix gently until all the ingredients have been combined.

Line a muffin tray with paper cases and divide the mixture evenly between them. You can use an ice-cream scoop to make the muffins the same size. Scatter over the pumpkin seeds. Bake in the oven for 20-25 minutes. When a wooden cocktail stick inserted into a muffin comes out clean, the muffins are cooked. Remove from the oven and leave them to cool.

Once cooked, you'll notice that their vibrant pink colour has faded – this is normal.

TIP:
You can take the muffins with you for a quick lunch or serve them with a salad and some Cashew Soured Cream (see page 17).

PICKLES

The process of making pickles is one of the oldest methods of food preserving. There are two ways of pickling: with vinegar or with salt. The term pickling actually comes from the Dutch word '*pekel*' (brine in English), which means 'salt'. By preserving food this way, Dutch navigators could easily take supplies with them on their ships. But 'pickling' is not typically Dutch; think of German sauerkraut, Korean kimchi, Japanese tsukemono and olives. Pickles make a delicious side dish to heavier and fatty dishes. Flavour-wise, I think they make a meal far more interesting.

RED ONION PICKLE – Makes a 500ml jar

4 medium red onions
½ teaspoon coriander seeds
½ teaspoon black peppercorns

½ teaspoon salt
200ml raw apple cider vinegar

Peel the onions and thinly slice them into half-moons (you can use a mandoline for this). Place them in a 500ml glass jar with a well-fitting lid, packing them in tightly. Add the spices and salt, pour in the vinegar and top it up with water. Seal the jar and leave for at least 3–4 hours or, better still, overnight. The pickle will keep for a month in the fridge.

SPICY CARROT PICKLE – Makes two 500ml jars

500g (rainbow) carrots
1 teaspoon cumin seeds
2 garlic cloves, roughly chopped
2cm piece of ginger, peeled and roughly
  chopped

1 red chilli, deseeded and sliced
250ml water
250ml raw apple cider vinegar
¾ teaspoon salt

Start by scrubbing the carrots and washing them. Cut them into a shape you desire; I like either julienne or thin rounds. Toast your cumin seeds for a minute or so in a dry pan over a low heat until they are fragrant. Take the seeds out of the pan and divide between two 500ml glass jars with well-fitting lids. Add the garlic, ginger and chilli to the jars then the carrots. Combine the water, vinegar and salt in a large pan and bring it to a gentle boil. Mix until the salt has dissolved. Pour this liquid over your two jars leaving about a 1.5cm gap at the top. You may not have to use all of your liquid. Seal the jars and shake them to remove any air pockets. Leave to cool and store in the fridge. The pickle needs 2–3 days to develop flavour and will last at least a month in your fridge.

LASAGNE WITH LENTIL RAGOUT AND CAULIFLOWER BÉCHAMEL

Lasagne is a crowd-pleasing dish with its comforting flavours. It's perfect for when guests are coming – you can prepare the lasagne ahead of time and pop it in the oven when they arrive. I swapped the traditional meat-based sauce for a lentil and tomato ragout and the milk-based béchamel for a creamy cashew sauce.

Serves 6

250g dried lasagne sheets of your choice
  (spelt, wholegrain, gluten-free)

for the lentil ragout
2 carrots, grated
1 onion, finely diced
250g mushrooms, roughly chopped
1 courgette, grated
5 garlic cloves, chopped
½ teaspoon chilli powder (or more, to taste)
700ml tomato passata
1 tablespoon mushroom powder (see Tip,
  page 15)
1 tablespoon maple syrup (optional)

500g (drained weight) cooked, lentils (either
  homemade or from two 400g cans)
2 teaspoons dried oregano
1 bunch of fresh basil, roughly chopped
300ml vegetable stock (see page 14) or water
salt, to taste

for the béchamel
400g cauliflower florets
200g cashews, soaked and drained
200ml vegetable stock (see page 14) or hot water
3 tablespoons nutritional yeast
¼–½ teaspoon freshly grated nutmeg (to taste)
salt

Preheat the oven to 180°C/gas mark 4.

To make the ragout, heat a large non-stick frying pan and add the carrots, onion, mushrooms and courgette. Water fry them with 2 tablespoons of water or stock. Sauté until the vegetables are soft and translucent (this will take about 8–10 minutes). Then stir in the garlic and chilli, and cook for a further 2 minutes. Now add the passata, mushroom powder, maple syrup, lentils, oregano, basil, vegetable stock and salt to taste. Bring to the boil, then simmer over a low heat for about 15–20 minutes.

Meanwhile, make the béchamel. Start by adding the cauliflower florets to a pan of boiling water and cook until they are soft (they are done when

you can easily pierce one with a sharp knife). Drain the florets and transfer to a blender. Add the soaked cashews, vegetable stock, nutritional yeast, salt and nutmeg. Blend until completely smooth. Set aside.

When the ragout is ready you can assemble your lasagne. Take a large deep-sided ovenproof dish (mine is 20 x 30cm) and spread a little ragout over the base. Form a layer of lasagne sheets then a layer of ragout. Continue to layer the lasagne sheets and ragout until the dish is almost full and you have used up all the ragout. Top the lasagne with the béchamel and transfer the dish to the middle of your oven. Cook for 45 minutes then remove from the oven. Let it sit for 10 minutes before serving.

PEANUT AND SWEET POTATO SOUP

Peanut soup is a popular dish in Indonesian and Surinam restaurants in the Netherlands, but it originates from Africa and is very well known in countries like Ghana, Nigeria and Gambia. Usually it is a soup or a stew made of ground peanuts, tomatoes, other vegetables and often chicken, served with rice, millet or sweet potatoes. My version is made with peanut butter and, instead of serving the soup with sweet potatoes, I use them in the soup itself. Make sure you use a good-quality peanut butter that only contains peanuts and salt. Avoid ones using palm oil and sugar.

Serves 4 as a main, 6-8 as a starter or lunch

1 teaspoon cumin seeds
1 teaspoon coriander seeds
1 onion, diced
4-5 garlic cloves
½ teaspoon ground cinnamon
½ teaspoon allspice
1 red chilli, deseeded and chopped
2-3 tomatoes, chopped
600g sweet potato, peeled and diced into
  2cm cubes
120ml peanut butter
1 litre vegetable stock (see page 14) or water

100g kale or cavolo nero, torn
220g (drained weight) cooked black lentils or
  black beans, (see page 32) or from a 440g jar/
  can, drained
salt

for the topping
100ml Cashew Soured Cream (see page 17)
  or coconut yogurt
fresh coriander, chopped
fresh chilli, chopped

Roast the cumin and coriander seeds in a large dry frying pan until fragrant. Add the onions and a splash of water or stock. Sauté until the onions are translucent (this will take 4-5 minutes). If needed, add a bit more liquid. Now add the garlic, cinnamon, allspice, chilli, tomatoes and sweet potato and stir until all the ingredients are covered. Cook for a further 2 minutes and then add the peanut butter – you need to work fast otherwise the peanut butter will stick to the pan. Stir until the peanut butter has dissolved.

Pour in the stock and bring to the boil. Leave to simmer over a medium heat for 18-20 minutes until the sweet potato is soft and cooked. Purée the soup in a blender or with an immersion blender until smooth. Return the soup to the pan and add the kale and beans. Cook for a further 2-4 minutes until the kale has wilted and the beans are warm. Add salt to taste and serve in bowls with a swirl of cashew soured cream and topped with fresh coriander and chilli. The soup also freezes well.

TIP:
Sprinkle almond and sesame topping (see page 24) over the soup for extra flavour. You can add cooked grains like rice or quinoa to the soup as well.

CRUNCHY SALAD WITH AVOCADO HERBED DRESSING

This salad isn't new, in fact it is based on two famous recipes: Waldorf salad and Green Goddess dressing. The first was created in the Waldorf Astoria hotel in New York back in 1896 and originally had celery, walnuts, apples and grapes dressed in mayonnaise. The Green Goddess dressing was created in the Palace hotel in San Francisco in 1923, and its original ingredients were spring onions, parsley, tarragon, anchovies and mayonnaise. Of course, here I omit the anchovies and make an egg-free mayonnaise.

Serves 4

For the salad

5 celery sticks, thinly sliced
2 fennel bulbs, thinly sliced
2 green apples, quartered, cored and thinly sliced
150g salad leaves, such as watercress

for the dressing

1 ripe avocado, halved and stoned
120ml natural plant-based yogurt
1–2 garlic cloves
3 tablespoons raw apple cider vinegar
3 tablespoons chopped parsley, chives and dill
½ teaspoon salt or white miso, to taste
freshly ground black pepper

Blend all the dressing ingredients in a blender until smooth. Check the seasoning then pour the dressing into a bowl.

Combine the salad ingredients in a large bowl or on a plate. Serve the salad with the dressing on top.

TIP:
You can use the Maple Mustard Topping (see page 25) for some extra crunch.

WHOLE ROASTED CAULIFLOWER, SPICED RICE AND FRESH GREEN CHUTNEY

Cauliflower rice, cauliflower steak, cauliflower wings, cauliflower purée, cauliflower pasta sauce...
who knew this humble veg was going to be such a hip ingredient? And for a good reason; you can
do a lot with cauliflower, because it tastes quite mild and adapts easily to any flavourings you give it.
I really like to serve a whole roasted cauliflower as a centrepiece when having guests.

Serves 4

1 whole cauliflower, outer leaves
  removed
1 teaspoon cumin seeds
1 teaspoon coriander seeds
½ teaspoon fennel seeds
1 teaspoon mustard seeds (optional)
1 teaspoon garam masala
1 teaspoon your favourite curry blend
1 teaspoon chilli powder
1 tablespoon fresh chopped ginger
1 onion, finely chopped
400g can peeled tomatoes, chopped
3 tablespoons fresh chopped coriander, to serve
salt

for the rice
1 cinnamon stick
½ teaspoon whole cloves
8 whole cardamom pods
300g brown basmati rice, washed
1 bay leaf
600ml vegetable stock or water

for the chutney
bunch of fresh coriander, chopped
bunch of fresh mint, chopped
juice of ½ lemon or lime
½ teaspoon cumin seeds
1 green chilli, seeds removed (leave them
  in if you like it hot)
1 garlic clove, chopped
2 spring onions, chopped
3 tablespoons coconut yogurt
½ teaspoon salt

Preheat the oven to 180°C/gas mark 4. Remove the stem and part of the core of the cauliflower – be careful not to remove too much as the core keeps the cauliflower together.

Roast the cumin, coriander, fennel and mustard seeds (if using) in a dry pan over a low heat until fragrant. Add the garam masala, curry powder, fresh ginger, onion and 3 tablespoons water or stock. Stir-fry this mixture over a medium heat until the onion is soft and translucent. Then

add the tomatoes, bring to the boil and leave to simmer over a low heat for 10 minutes.

Place your cauliflower, cored side down, in a deep ovenproof dish or cast-iron pan and pour over the sauce. Put the lid on the pan or cover the cauliflower with a sheet of foil. Cook for 60 minutes, then uncover and cook for a further 30 minutes or until the cauliflower is cooked. You can test this by piercing it with a sharp knife.

continued ⟶

⟶ Meanwhile make the rice. Roast the cinnamon, cloves and cardamom in a small dry pan over a medium heat until fragrant. Add the basmati rice to a large pan with the bay leaf, the roasted spices and the vegetable stock or water. Cook the rice according to the instructions on the packet. Once cooked, remove from the heat and set aside with the lid on.

Make the chutney by pulse chopping the chutney ingredients in a food processor. You want a chutney that is quite smooth, almost like a pesto. Set aside.

Once the cauliflower is cooked, scatter over some of the fresh coriander. Serve the cauliflower with the rice and chutney.

TIP:
Because the roasted cauliflower itself is quite subtle in flavour, you can transform it to any taste you like. Rub the cauliflower with a mixture of 2–3 tablespoons of tomato purée, harissa to taste and a squeeze of lemon juice for a more North African feel. Use 2 tablespoons of curry paste, 1 teaspoon of lime juice and some coconut milk for an Asian-inspired cauliflower. Thin the umami paste from page 15 with some water or rice vinegar (so it resembles mayonnaise) for a Japanese-style cauliflower and make a South American version with the chimichurri from page 76.

ROAST PUMPKIN

My favourite way of preparing pumpkin or squash is to roast them in the oven. Because I don't use a lot of oil in my cooking (see page 10), when roasting pumpkin I substitute it with balsamic vinegar, orange juice, stock or water. I often make a big batch of roast pumpkin for the whole week so that I can make a quick and healthy meal on days when I have less time. I use the roasted pumpkin in salads, soups, grain bowls, pasta dishes and for packed lunches.

Serves 4 as a main

1 pumpkin or squash weighing 1 1.5kg, such as
  butternut, red kuri or kabocha
2 red onions, peeled
1 teaspoon chilli flakes

1 teaspoon sea salt
2-3 tablespoons white balsamic vinegar,
  vegetable stock or water

Preheat the oven to 200°C/gas mark 6 and line a baking tray with baking paper.

Halve and then quarter the pumpkin and remove the seeds with a spoon. Peel off the skin with a small knife or a swivel-head peeler. Now cut the pumpkin into 2-3cm cubes. Cut the onions into 1-2cm dice. Transfer the pumpkin and onion to a large bowl and add the chilli flakes, sea salt and the liquid of choice. Mix the vegetables until they are all coated with the spices, salt and liquid. Spread out the pumpkin mix on the lined tray allowing enough space around the cubes for them to cook evenly. Bake for about 25-30 minutes in the middle of the oven, turning halfway through the cooking time. The pumpkin is done when it is soft but still hold its shape. Use directly or cool and store in the fridge.

GRILLED RADICCHIO, BAKED PUMPKIN, BEAN PURÉE AND GREMOLATA

Gremolata is a mixture of lemon zest, garlic and parsley. Italians will know it for its use in the meat dish *ossobucco*, but I think it goes very well with vegetables too, for example this autumn recipe of radicchio, pumpkin and beans.

Serves 4

450ml vegetable stock (see page 14)
450g white beans (drained weight) either home
  cooked or from two 440g cans
head of radicchio, sliced into 8 wedges
1–2 tablespoons balsamic vinegar
½ quantity of Roast Pumpkin (see page 53),
  cut into wedges
salt and freshly ground black pepper

For the gremolata
1 teaspoon lemon zest
small bunch of parsley, chopped
1 garlic clove, finely grated
Maple and Mustard Topping (see page 25),
  to serve

Preheat the grill to 200°C/gas mark 6 and line a baking tray with baking paper. Put the stock in a medium pan and bring to the boil. Add the beans and leave to simmer for 5–7 minutes. Then take out the beans and add them to a blender with about 100ml stock. Blend until smooth, adding a bit more stock if necessary, but be careful not to add too much liquid   you want it the same consistency as mashed potato. (You can also mash the beans with a potato masher; this will give it a more rustic look.) Taste and add salt and pepper if needed. Return the beans to the pan and keep them warm on a very low heat, stirring from time to time to prevent burning. The leftover stock can be discarded.

While the beans are cooking, lay the radicchio wedges on the lined tray. Sprinkle over the balsamic vinegar and add salt and pepper.

Grill the wedges for 5–6 minutes, turning them regularly so that they don't burn.

Make the gremolata by mixing the lemon zest, parsley, lemon zest and garlic with a good pinch of salt in a bowl.

When the radicchio wedges are cooked you can start plating. Begin by adding a bit of bean purée to the individual plates, add the grilled radicchio and pumpkin chunks on top, then sprinkle over some of the gremolata and the maple and mustard topping. Ready to be served!

TIP:
This is great served with the balsamic reduction on page 86.

SPRING VEGETABLES PARCELS

Cooking *en papillotte* is the French term for wrapping food in baking paper so that it steams in a hot oven. This method of preparing food is healthy and clean – you don't have to add any oil. I leave my guests to open the *papillottes* at the table so they can enjoy the release of the aromas and flavours of the vegetables.

Serves 4

2 lemons, cut into 8 slices
bunch of radishes, green stalks removed, and halved
bunch of green asparagus, woody ends trimmed, and cut into 3cm pieces
head of broccoli, cut into small florets
200g broad beans (defrosted if frozen)
1 small garlic clove, finely chopped (optional)

1 teaspoon chilli flakes (optional)
4 tablespoons water or vegetable stock (see page 14)

To serve
Cashew Soured Cream (see page 17)
small bunch of soft herbs – parsley, tarragon, dill or chives (or a mix of these), finely chopped

Preheat the oven to 200°C/gas mark 4. Cut four 30cm squares of baking paper and lay them open on your worktop. Place two slices of lemon on each sheet. In a large bowl combine the radishes, asparagus, broccoli and broad beans and add salt, garlic and chilli flakes (if using), to taste. Distribute the vegetables equally over the four sheets. Now bring the edges of the paper together to form a parcel and spoon 1 tablespoon of stock or water into each parcel. Bind the parcels with kitchen twine so they are completely enclosed at the top.

Place the four parcels on a baking tray and cook for 25 minutes. Open one parcel to see if your vegetables are cooked, they still should have a little bite. If they are not cooked, close the parcel again and cook them for a further 5 minutes. Serve with a dollop of cashew soured cream and scatter over some fresh chopped herbs.

TIP:
I like to serve the parcels with new potatoes or polenta.

WHOLEGRAIN PANCAKES WITH CHERRY COMPOTE

Pancakes, or *Pannenkoeken*, as we call them have a special place in Dutch food culture. Having pancakes at a party or for dinner is seen as a real treat. Ask a Dutch child what would be good to eat for dinner and probably it will be pancakes with apple syrup or sugar. My girl doesn't agree at all with the traditional Dutch pancakes; in fact, I always have to make something different for her if pancakes are eaten on special occasions. The ones she really likes are small American-style pancakes, which I sometimes serve for breakfast. This recipe makes quite a few pancakes, because I like to freeze them. Then, during the week, I can grab some from the freezer and reheat them in the oven.

Makes 20–22 pancakes (10cm diameter)

For the pancakes
300g wholegrain (spelt) flour or use a
  gluten-free flour if you prefer
700ml plant-based milk
1½ teaspoon baking powder
pinch of salt
2 tablespoons chia seeds
3 tablespoons maple syrup

for the cherry compote
500g pitted cherries (defrosted if frozen)
juice of 2 orange
½ teaspoon vanilla powder
1 teaspoon ground ginger
2 teaspoons ground cinnamon
2 teaspoons arrowroot or cornflour
handful of chopped raw almonds, to serve

To make the pancake batter combine all the ingredients in a large bowl. Whisk until no lumps remain and set aside for 10 minutes (you can do this the night before and keep in the fridge).

Heat a non-stick frying pan when you are ready to cook the pancakes. Pour in 2 tablespoons of batter per pancake. Depending on the size of your pan, you can bake several at once. When small air holes appear and the surface of the pancakes is dry you can flip them. Now cook for a further 1–2 minutes on the other side. Keep them warm between two plates in the oven on the lowest temperature while you cook the rest.

While the pancakes cook, make the cherry compote. Put the cherries, orange juice, vanilla, ginger and cinnamon in a small pan over a low-medium heat. When the cherry compote starts to simmer, turn down the heat to low, and let it simmer for a further 5 minutes. Combine the arrowroot and 2 tablespoons of water in a small bowl. Mix this into your cherry compote and stir well. Leave to cook for 1 minute until the compote thickens.

Serve the pancakes with the cherry compote and some chopped almonds.

TIP:
If you would like to freeze any of your pancakes, stack them with baking paper between them so that it is easier to separate them.

WEEKDAYS

During the working week you have less time to spend on cooking but you still want something delicious and healthy and, if you have a family, you will want to give your kids the best you can. Nowadays a lot of people opt for so-called ready-meals from a supermarket because they are fast and easy, and there is no preparation. But these meals are full of fats and refined sugars, not many are vegan and they are expensive. In this chapter I will show you vegan dishes that take no longer than 30 minutes to prepare, dishes you can take with you or that can be eaten the next day. With some planning and preparation at the weekend you can eat vegan during the week as well. It is not complicated at all!

SPRING-GREEN CHICKPEA PIZZA

I don't always have the time or the patience to make a yeast-based pizza dough. You have to knead it, stretch it, shape it and leave it to rest. It takes time. So, in this recipe I use a chickpea crust. Now you only need to mix chickpea flour with some water and salt to make a dough. The name of this recipe sums up both the colour and the components of this wonderful pizza. It takes minimal effort for maximum result!

Serves 4 for a light lunch or 2 as a main

For the pizza
250g chickpea (gram) flour, sifted
1 teaspoon salt
1 courgette, cut lengthways into ribbons
½ bunch of green asparagus, cut into ribbons
3 spring onions, sliced into 0.5cm pieces
70g pitted green olives (optional)
2 tablespoons pine nuts
freshly ground black pepper

For the pesto sauce
large bunch of basil, chopped
  (reserve some leaves as garnish)
½ avocado, stoned and peeled
50g pine nuts
juice of ½ lemon
1 garlic clove, finely chopped
2 tablespoons nutritional yeast (optional)

Preheat the oven to its highest setting. Use a whisk to mix the chickpea flour with 500ml water, salt and some pepper in a large bowl. Keep stirring until no lumps remain. If you have 5 minutes to spare set it aside – this will improve the batter. Pour the mixture into a shallow baking tray (about 20 x 30cm). If the tray isn't non-stick, line the base with baking paper. Bake for 13–15 minutes until the pizza base has set.

Meanwhile, make the pesto in a food-processor by simply mixing all the ingredients until a sauce forms. If needed, add a splash of water to keep the machine going. Taste and adjust the seasoning if needed, then pour the pesto into a bowl and set aside.

When the pizza base is cooked, remove it from the oven and switch on the grill to high. Spread the basil pesto over the base and scatter the remaining ingredients on top. Place under the grill for 3–5 minutes. Keep an eye on the pizza to ensure the topping ingredients do not burn. Once everything is cooked it is ready to serve, garnished with the reserved basil.

PIPERADE

I love watching cooking shows, especially those on the BBC channels. I remember once watching an episode of Keith Floyd where he made piperade, a Basque dish of cooked onions, peppers and tomatoes, in the kitchen of a French woman. She wasn't impressed by his cooking and she told him clearly how she felt a real piperade should be made. She liked only the traditional version of this famous dish – not Keith's, and I don't think she would approve of my version either. Nonetheless, it's a perfectly delicious vegan variation of a classic.

Serves 2

250g block of medium-firm tofu,
   drained
2 red onions, diced
2 peppers, 1 red and 1 yellow, sliced
4 garlic cloves, finely chopped
4 medium tomatoes, chopped

pinch of turmeric (optional)
small bunch of flat-leaf parsley, chopped
salt (if possible kala namak, Indian black salt)
   and pepper
toasted bread, cooked grains or potatoes, to
   serve

Crumble the tofu with a fork in a bowl (it should end up looking like scrambled egg) and set aside.

Heat a non-stick or cast-iron pan over a high heat. Add the onions and fry with a touch of water (or stock if you have some). Cook until the onions are soft and golden, adding a little more liquid if needed. This takes about 5–7 minutes. Reduce the heat to medium and add the peppers, garlic and tomatoes. Mix together and let it cook for about 6–8 minutes to soften the peppers and tomatoes. Add the crumbled tofu, along with the turmeric (if using). Season with salt and pepper to taste. Cook for a further 1–2 minutes until the tofu is warmed through. Sprinkle with parsley and serve with toasted bread, cooked grains or potatoes for a more filling meal.

VEGAN 'EGG' SALADS

In the late seventies and eighties, egg salads were the fashionable thing to make when you threw a party. I remember watching my grandma making the salad every time we had a family get-together. In memory of these happy family occasions, I really wanted to create a vegan version of an egg salad. These salads are super easy to make and great on toast, in a wrap, served with grains and greens, etc. The trick is to use kala namak, which is Indian black salt, because this is what gives the dish its 'eggy' taste.

CHICKPEA CURRIED 'EGG' SALAD – Makes a filling for two wraps

220g (drained weight) cooked chickpeas from
  a 420g jar/can
1 generous teaspoon of your favourite curry
  blend

½ teaspoon kala namak (Indian black salt)
  or another good-quality salt
80ml natural plant-based yogurt

Roughly mash the beans with a fork in a bowl. Do not mash completely; you want to keep some texture. Add the curry, salt and yogurt and mix until combined. Stored in the fridge it will last for 3–4 days.

FRENCH-STYLE 'EGG' CANNELLINI SALAD – Makes a filling for two wraps

220g (drained weight) cooked cannellini or other
  white beans from a 420g jar/can
8 small gherkins (ensure they are sugar-free),
  finely chopped

1 shallot, finely chopped
1 teaspoon Dijon mustard
2 tablespoons chopped chives
½ teaspoon kala namak (Indian black salt)

Roughly mash the beans with a fork in a bowl. Do not mash completely; you want to keep some texture. Add the rest of the ingredients and mix until combined. Stored in the fridge it will last for 3–4 days.

SERVING SUGGESTIONS:
These bean salads make great fillings for wraps or sandwiches. When making a wrap, it is best to use a large salad leaf (or a bed of smaller greens) between the bean salad and the bread to prevents the bread from becoming soggy. I like to add some grated beetroot, carrot, thinly sliced cucumber, radishes, alfalfa sprouts, red onion pickle (see page 42) or avocado, too. If you want to take the wrap with you for lunch, fold it in some baking paper and tie it up.

DAHL WITH COCONUT TOPPING

This Indian red lentil dish is one of my daughter's favourite meals (by the way, she has a lot and they vary from time to time). There are some spices in here, but it is never too hot or too complex for a child's taste. The coconut topping is a good contrast to the soft lentils and makes this dish even more interesting. So much so that the two-year-old son of our neighbours whom we invited to dinner was still talking about it the day after he had tasted it. It is a perfect introduction to Indian cuisine for children.

Serves 4

2 onions, finely diced
3 garlic cloves, finely diced
3cm piece of fresh ginger, peeled and finely chopped or grated
1 teaspoon cumin seeds
½ teaspoon coriander seeds
2 teaspoons ground turmeric
½ teaspoon chilli flakes
250g red lentils, washed
750–850ml water or vegetable stock (see page 14)
75g spinach or chard
½ teaspoon salt (or more to taste)

for the topping
75g desiccated coconut (unsweetened)
1 teaspoon cumin seeds
1 teaspoon coriander seeds
1 teaspoon black mustard seeds (optional)

to serve
3 tablespoons chopped coriander
lemon wedges
Flatbreads (see page 27)

Add the onions and garlic to a large non-stick pan with a splash of water or stock. Sauté the onions until they are translucent. This will take about 3–4 minutes. Then add the ginger, spices and, if necessary, a little more water to stop it burning. Cook for a further minute. Add the lentils to the onion and spice mix and stir. Now pour in the water or stock. Bring to the boil then lower the heat and simmer for about 20 minutes until the red lentils are cooked. Add the spinach or chard and continue to cook for about 2 minutes or until the leaves have wilted. Add salt to taste.

Meanwhile, make the coconut topping. Dry-roast the coconut and spices in a dry non-stick or cast-iron pan over a low heat, stirring frequently. Coconut burns easily, so stay with your pan. When the coconut is golden brown it is ready. Transfer the mixture to a bowl.

Scatter the dahl with the coconut topping and serve it with fresh coriander, lemon wedges and flatbreads.

TIP:
Any leftover dahl makes for an easy lunch the following day. It is delicious if you pair it with some grains and pickles

SPINACH GALETTE WITH MUSHROOM RAGOUT

French cuisine is not known for being vegan-friendly. That said, the French are widely known for their fine cooking and should not be excluded. One of their more vegan-friendly dishes (it all depends on the filling) is Brittany's galette. This pancake is made with buckwheat flour and water and often has a savoury filling. My recipe is a nice twist on the classic dish because I added spinach to the batter. Here the galette is served with one of its classic toppings: creamy mushrooms. They go so well with the taste of the buckwheat galette.

Serves 4

for the galettes
200g buckwheat flour (or use wholegrain)
350ml water or plant-based milk
100g spinach (or kale stripped from its stems), washed
1 tablespoon ground linseeds
salt, to taste

for the filling
1 medium onion, finely chopped or sliced
750g mixed mushrooms (chanterelle, oyster or shiitake), cleaned and torn up

1 teaspoon fresh thyme leaves
3 garlic cloves, finely chopped
1 teaspoon mushroom powder (see page 15)
½ small bunch of chopped fresh flat-leaf parsley, sage or oregano leaves
100ml Cashew Soured Cream (see page 17) or shop-bought oat cream
salt and freshly ground black pepper, to taste
salad leaves, such as rocket, watercress or baby spinach, to serve

---

Start by making the galette. Blend all the ingredients in a blender, or put in a large bowl and mix using an immersion blender. Allow the batter to rest for 5–10 minutes.

To make the mushroom filling, heat a non-stick pan and add the onions. Add a small splash of water and cook until translucent. Then add the mushrooms, thyme, garlic, mushroom powder and salt and pepper. Cook for about 8–10 minutes, adding a little more water if needed to prevent it burning.

While the mushrooms are simmering, make the galettes. Heat a non-stick 24cm pan over a medium heat. Pour in about 60–80ml of the mix and spread out quickly – you want your galette to be thin. Let it cook until the surface is dry and

the base will come easily away from the pan. When the surface of the galette is dry, flip it over and cook the other side for a minute or so. (If you flip it too soon, the galette will break or stick. This is the tricky part of baking the perfect galette.) Repeat until all the batter has been used. Keep the galettes warm between two plates in the oven on a low temperature.

When the mushrooms are cooked, taste and add more seasoning if needed. Now add the fresh herbs and the cashew soured cream or oat cream and stir until combined.

Spread some mushroom ragout over the spinach galettes and fold each one in half. Serve with a few salad leaves. *Bon appétit!*

FIVE VEGETABLE TAGINE

My French sister-in-law introduced me to a Moroccan-inspired vegetable tagine. The first time she cooked this for me, she used turnips and pumpkin as well as other vegetables. I really liked it and since then it has been part of my repertoire as well. I always use seasonal vegetables for tagine, but feel free to experiment.

Serves 4-6

2 red onions, peeled and chopped
300ml vegetable stock (see page 14)
1 teaspoon coriander seeds
1 teaspoon cumin seeds
1 cinnamon stick
½ teaspoon ground turmeric
1½ tablespoons harissa paste, plus extra to serve
1 thumb-sized piece of fresh ginger, peeled and chopped
1 bay leaf
rind of 1 lemon
3 carrots, cut into 2cm slices
1 aubergine, chopped into 3cm chunks

2 medium sweet potatoes, chopped into 3cm chunks
400g can of tomatoes, chopped
220g (drained weight) cooked chickpeas from a 420g jar/can
handful of raisins
wholegrain couscous, bulgur wheat or quinoa
salt

to serve
3 tablespoons freshly chopped mint
75g chopped almonds

Add the onions to a large non-stick pan with a splash of water or a little of the stock. Sauté the onions until they are soft and translucent. This will take about 3-4 minutes. Then add the spices, harissa, ginger, bay leaf, lemon and the vegetables. Cook and stir for 1 minute and, if needed, add a few tablespoons of water or stock. Now add the tomatoes and the rest of the stock, chickpeas and raisins. Bring to the boil and leave to simmer for 15-20 minutes until the vegetables are soft. Taste and add salt as needed.

Meanwhile, cook your grains according to the instructions on the packet.

Serve the tagine with the chopped mint, almonds and extra harissa to taste.

GREEN MINESTRONE WITH MARJORAM PESTO

While renovating our home in the depths of winter we did not have any heating. I would often make a classic minestrone to keep us warm and energised. The classic version of this soup is made with tomatoes, but when spring comes and the new season's vegetables are available, I feel like having a lighter soup based on fresh greens and herbs.

Serves 4

bunch of spring onions, roughly chopped
5 garlic cloves, chopped
3 celery sticks, chopped
2 litres vegetable stock (see page 14) or water
1½ tablespoons chopped thyme
1 tablespoon chopped rosemary
3 medium potatoes, peeled and diced
1 courgette, diced
1 fennel bulb, diced
2 teaspoons mushroom powder (see page 15)
1 bay leaf, cracked
200g broad beans (defrosted if frozen)
200g peas (defrosted if frozen)

For the pesto
35g pine nuts
35g walnuts
bunch of marjoram (or oregano), and chopped
bunch of basil, chopped
1 garlic clove, chopped
1 avocado, halved, stoned and chopped
1 tablespoon nutritional yeast
½ teaspoon maple syrup
zest and juice of 1 lemon
salt

Add the onions, garlic and celery to a large non-stick pan with a splash of water or a little of the stock. Sauté until they are soft and translucent. This will take about 3–4 minutes. If necessary, add a little more water to stop it burning.

Meanwhile, bring the stock or water to the boil in a separate pan. Add the herbs, potatoes, courgette, fennel, mushroom powder and bay leaf to the onion mixture then pour in the stock. Bring back to the boil then turn down the heat and simmer for 10 minutes. Add the broad beans and cook for a further 5 minutes. At the very last minute, add the peas. Taste, and add salt and pepper if needed.

While the soup is cooking, make the pesto using a pestle and mortar or a small food processor. Just combine all ingredients and grind or blitz to a smooth consistency. Taste, and add extra salt if needed. The pesto should taste a bit on the salty side, but this will be diluted in the soup.

Serve the soup with a dollop of pesto in each bowl and some wholegrain sourdough on the side.

TIP:
This soup freezes very well, so you can make this in advance or make a big batch and freeze in individual portions.

FENNEL AND LEMON STEW

Wild fennel grows abundantly in my garden in France. The moment the fennel flowers or seedheads form, I pick some and start making a recipe with them. Fennel has a distinctive sweet smell and fresh flavour, reminiscent of aniseed and liquorice, which I just adore, and it pairs fantastically with lemon. This easy and rustic stew can be made in late summer when the fennel bulbs are just large enough, in autumn and even in early winter, because both lemons and fennel will still be available. These flavours will make you dream of hot and sunny days even when it's cold outside!

Serves 2 as a main or 4 as a side dish

500g fennel bulbs
2 bay leaves
3 garlic cloves, crushed
5 lemon slices
450ml vegetable stock (see page 14) or water
400g potatoes (you want a variety that keeps its shape, such as Charlotte), sliced
½ teaspoon chilli flakes (or more, to taste), plus extra to serve

240g (drained weight) cooked butter beans from a 400g jar or can
70g pitted good-quality black olives, such as Kalamata
3 tablespoons chopped flat-leaf parsley, to serve

Wash the fennel and cut off the stalks and green tops (keep the feathery tops as garnish). Slice the fennel bulbs from top to bottom into thin wedges. Put the slices in a pan with the bay leaves, garlic, lemon, stock, potatoes and chilli. Bring to the boil, then turn down the heat and simmer for 15 minutes. Add the butter beans and olives. Continue to simmer for a further 5–7 minutes until the fennel is soft and the potatoes cooked. Serve with the fennel tops, parsley and a few extra chilli flakes.

TIP:
For a more filling meal, serve the stew with cooked grains, polenta, a nice slice of sourdough or even wholegrain pasta.

BRUSSELS SPROUTS STIR-FRY WITH SPICY PUMPKIN SEEDS

Ask anyone about their least favourite vegetable and there is a good chance the answer will be Brussels sprouts. In my opinion, sprouts have this bad reputation because they are often overcooked and then start smelling too strongly. But when quickly blanched or stir-fried, sprouts smell less, the texture is crisper and the taste is far superior. Combined with smoky tofu, the citrus tang of the orange and the earthy tones of the buckwheat, these Brussels sprouts won't disappoint.

Serves 4

1 leek, trimmed, washed and thinly sliced
2 carrots, sliced into matchsticks (or try this
  on a mandoline or food processor)
1 red chilli, thinly sliced (deseeded if you
  want less heat), some reserved for garnish
400g Brussels sprouts, thinly sliced (on a
  mandoline) or shredded in a food processor
4–5 garlic cloves, chopped finely
200g smoked tofu, cut into small cubes or strips
350g buckwheat or other noodles of choice
small bunch of spring onions, finely chopped,
  to serve

for the stir-fry sauce
juice of 1 orange
3 tablespoons shoyu or tamari sauce
1½ tablespoons balsamic vinegar
1 tablespoon maple syrup
2 teaspoons freshly grated ginger
2 tablespoons water
1 tablespoon cornflour or arrowroot

for the spicy pumpkin seeds
70g raw pumpkin seeds
1 tablespoon maple syrup
½ teaspoon chilli powder
1 tablespoon shoyu or tamari sauce

First, make the spicy pumpkin seeds. Heat a dry non-stick or cast-iron pan and roast the pumpkin seeds until they start to pop. Stir in the maple syrup and the chilli powder and fry for 30 seconds, then add the shoyu sauce. Stir, then transfer to a sheet of baking paper, spreading them out. Set aside to cool.

Make the stir-fry sauce by combining all the ingredients in a small bowl. Set aside.

Heat a wok or a large frying pan. You want to get the pan really hot to stir-fry the vegetables. Add the leek, carrot, chilli and Brussels sprouts. Don't start stirring too soon – you want the vegetables to have a nice caramelised layer, but keep an eye on them so that they don't burn. As soon as the veg have developed a little crust, stir and leave them frying. Add the garlic and, when needed, a splash of water or stock to prevent it burning. Stir again. The vegetables should retain some crunch, so the whole process of stir-frying on a high heat will take just 2–3 minutes. Now add the tofu and stir in the sauce. Allow the sauce to thicken – this will take less than a minute.

Meanwhile, cook the noodles according to the packet instructions, then rinse and drain.

Serve the stir-fried vegetables on the noodles and scatter over the pumpkin seeds, spring onions and some extra fresh chilli.

WINTER TABBOULEH WITH SPICY ZHOUG YOGURT SAUCE

Winter produce doesn't have to be dull. Sometimes you just have to be inventive to make seasonal versions of the dishes you like. In summer, tabbouleh would include tomatoes, but who wants to eat out of season vegetables that have no flavour? Not me. So I've swapped the tomatoes for grapefruits and added kale to this version.

Serves 4–6

For the tabbouleh
250g buckwheat
150g kale, washed, stripped off the stems
   and finely shredded or chopped
2 grapefruits, peeled and segmented (catch the
   juice in a small bowl while segmenting the fruit)
½ bunch of mint, washed and finely chopped
bunch of flat-leaf parsley, washed and finely
   chopped
100g pumpkin seeds
1 teaspoon coriander seeds
60g dried cranberries (ensure they are
   sugar-free)
salt, to taste

For the zhoug
5 jalapeño peppers (or 7 for extra heat), chopped
bunch of coriander, chopped
small bunch of flat-leaf parsley, chopped
2–3 garlic cloves, chopped
¾ teaspoon coriander powder
¾ teaspoon cumin powder
¾ teaspoon cardamom powder
juice of ½ lemon
80ml natural plant-based yogurt, plus extra
   to serve
salt

Start by bringing 1.5 litres of water to the boil in a large pan. Add the buckwheat and cook for about 18 minutes – it needs to retain some bite. When cooked, drain and rinse under the tap and drain again in a colander

Meanwhile, dry-roast the pumpkin seeds in a small dry pan over a low heat until they start to pop, then set aside. Use the same pan to dry roast the coriander seeds until fragrant and set aside too.

Next make the zhoug. Combine all the ingredients and blitz in a food processor until it has the consistency of pesto. Add salt to taste. Set aside.

Combine the drained buckwheat, kale, grapefruit segments and juice, herbs, the pumpkin and coriander seeds and the cranberries in a large bowl. Taste and add more salt if needed.

Serve the tabbouleh with the zhoug sauce. If the sauce is too hot, stir some of it into a small bowl of plant-based yogurt.

TIP:
Winter Tabbouleh is fantastic with the falafel burgers in this chapter (see page 78). The salad can be made in advance, it will keep for several days in the fridge and it's great to take to work with you for lunch.

GRILLED AVOCADO WITH RED CHIMICHURRI

Chimichurri is an uncooked sauce that originates from Argentina and Uruguay. There are two versions: one green, *chimichurri verde*, and one red, *chimichurri rojo*. It is often used as a marinade for grilled meat, or it will be pasted on the meat as it cooks. You can also serve chimichurri as a side dish, as I will be doing. Here is my recipe for a red chimichurri with grilled avocado, which you can cook on your barbecue

Serves 2 as a light lunch or 4 as a starter

2 ripe but still slightly firm avocados, halved
  and stoned
240g (drained weight) pinto beans (or red kidney
  beans) from a 420g jar/can, rinsed

For the chimichurri
1 red pepper, deseeded and roughly
  chopped
2 medium tomatoes (or 250g cherry tomatoes)
1 small red onion, chopped roughly
½ red chilli, deseeded and sliced

3 garlic cloves, chopped
1 teaspoon ground cumin
1½ teaspoons dried oregano
small bunch of fresh coriander, roughly
  chopped
small bunch of flat-leaf parsley, roughly
  chopped roughly
30ml raw apple cider vinegar
salt, to taste

Place a griddle pan over a high heat or use a barbecue. Put all the ingredients for the chimichurri in a food-processor and pulse-chop until reasonably smooth (it should still have some texture; it is not meant to be a soup). Transfer the chimichurri to a bowl and set aside.

Place the avocado halves on the griddlepan, cut-side down. Grill for about 3 minutes or until grill marks appear. Remove from the griddle or barbecue. Spoon some of the beans into the avocado centres and top with chimichurri. Done!

FALAFEL BURGERS WITH TAHINI SAUCE

When I was living in Amsterdam in my early twenties, little falafel shops opened everywhere. I was vegetarian at the time and it meant I could buy a delicious fast and easy snack just around the corner. If I skipped the yogurt sauce it was even vegan! Later on I learned about the dangers of deep frying and, because falafel from the shop was fried, I decided to make my own version baked in the oven. If you have a fan oven setting, do use it as this will give your falafel a nice crust without the use of any oil.

Serves 4

480g (drained weight) cooked chickpeas, homemade or from two 420g jars/cans
bunch of flat-leaf parsley, chopped
bunch of coriander, chopped
½ bunch of mint, leaves stripped from the stems and chopped
2 teaspoons ground cumin
1 teaspoon chilli powder
3–4 garlic cloves, chopped
1 teaspoon lemon zest and 1 tablespoon lemon juice
1 tablespoon tahini

2 Medjool dates, stoned and roughly chopped
4–6 tablespoons chickpea (gram) or other flour

For the tahini sauce
250ml tahini or sesame sauce
juice of 1½ lemons
150ml water (or more, depending on how thin you like the sauce)
3 garlic cloves (or less, to taste)
½ teaspoon ground cumin (optional)
1 teaspoon maple syrup
salt, to taste

Preheat the oven to 220°C fan/240°C/gas mark 9 and line a baking tray with baking paper.

Make the burgers by putting all the ingredients except the flour in the bowl of a food processor. Pulse-blend the mixture a few times and then add 4 tablespoons of flour. Pulse again until semi-smooth. To test if the mixture is the right consistency, take a small amount and try to form it into a ball. The mixture should hold its shape; if it is too wet add a bit of flour and, if it's too dry, add 1 or 2 tablespoons of water and mix again. The end-result should not be completely smooth, because it needs to have some chunks remaining, which gives the burgers more crunch.

Transfer the falafel mixture to a large bowl. Divide the mixture into four equal parts and shape the burgers with your hands. Transfer them to the lined tray and bake for 18–20 minutes in the middle of the oven.

Meanwhile, make the sauce by combining all the ingredients in a blender. Mix until smooth.

Serve with a flatbread, bun or wholegrain pitta bread, fresh salad leaves, sliced radishes, cooked beetroot, carrot or onion pickle (see page 42), hummus (see page 119), homemade ketchup (see page 22), zhoug (see page 75), etc.

TIP:
Both sauce and falafel can be stored in the fridge for 2–3 days. You can freeze the leftovers and take them out when you need them.

CELERIAC SALAD

I have spent many holidays in the Ardèche region of France. Although most tourists go there to enjoy its hot summers, autumn is a lovely season too, especially when the chestnut harvest begins. The Ardèche is justly famous for its chestnuts. In October you can buy them cheaply on the local market stalls, I even found local pomegranates on sale back then. Sweet chestnuts and crispy pomegranate seeds go very well with the nutty, earthy taste of celeriac and the bitter radicchio leaves. If you can't get chestnuts, walnuts will work well instead. All flavours are represented here and, in my mind, that makes it the perfect autumn salad.

Serves 4

150g (drained weight) cooked Puy or beluga lentils homemade (see page 32) or from a jar/can rinsed

4 cooked celeriac slices or steaks (see pages 37 and 38), cut into small cubes

75g watercress

1 head of red radicchio, finely shredded

100g cooked chestnuts (or walnuts), broken up a little

1 small raw (chioggia/candy striped) beetroot, julienned or grated

seeds from 1 pomegranate

bunch of flat-leaf parsley, washed and roughly chopped

For the dressing

200ml Cashew Soured Cream (see page 17) or natural plant-based yogurt

1 tablespoon raw apple cider vinegar

2 teaspoons wholegrain mustard

1 garlic clove, finely chopped

½ teaspoon maple syrup

½ teaspoon salt

First, make the dressing by combining all the ingredients in a small bowl. In another bowl, mix the dressing with the lentils and the celeriac, then set aside.

Place the watercress and radicchio on a large plate and top with the dressed lentils and celeriac. Scatter over the cooked chestnuts, beetroot, pomegranate seeds and parsley. Serve as it is or, for a more filling meal, with wholegrain sourdough bread, some cooked potatoes or cooked grains.

> **TIP:**
> This salad is perfect to take with you for a lunch at your desk. Start by filling a mason jar with the celeriac, lentils and sauce. Then add the chestnuts, beetroot, parsley and pomegranate seeds. Top with the watercress and red radicchio.

'NO TUNA' SUNFLOWER PÂTÉ IN SALAD CUPS

According to the latest research, wild fish in the oceans are rapidly becoming extinct. It is high time to switch to plant-based alternatives, like this fishless 'no tuna' pâté made from sunflower seeds.

Serves 4

for the pâté
150g sunflower seeds, soaked and drained
8 small gherkins, chopped
2 teaspoons chopped capers
1 small shallot, chopped
1 teaspoon Dijon mustard
1 teaspoon lemon juice
60–80ml natural plant-based yogurt or Cashew
  Soured Cream (see page 17)

for the salad cups
1 small head of Romaine or Little Gem lettuce,
  washed and leaves separated

250g cherry tomatoes, halved (or use
  multicoloured tomatoes or the slow-roasted
  tomatoes, see page 30)
½ cucumber, sliced into thin rounds
1 red pepper, deseeded and thinly sliced
75g pitted black olives, halved
3 tablespoons freshly chopped soft herbs, such
  as flat-leaf parsley, basil, chives, dill
1 lemon, cut into wedges
salt

Put all the ingredients for the pâté in a food-processor and process to a fine texture. Taste to check whether it needs more salt and add to your liking, you want it to taste a little salty. Transfer the mixture to a bowl.

Arrange the salad leaves on a plate, place a dollop of the pâté inside each leaf. Then top with the cherry tomatoes, cucumber, red pepper and olives. Scatter with the chopped herbs and serve with the lemon wedges to squeeze over the leaves.

> TIPS:
> The 'No tuna' pâté can easily be made in advance and can be stored in the fridge for 3–4 days. With some fresh tomatoes and cashew mozzarella (see page 18), it is very delicious sandwiched between two grilled slices of bread; the Americans call this a 'tuna melt'. Alternatively, try stirring the 'No tuna' pâté into pasta with grated courgette and blanched peas for a great, super-simple dinner.

CUP-A-NOODLES

Instant noodles can be bought in many Asian stores in Holland, as in most parts of the world. I used to buy them and enjoyed them as a quick snack. It's so easy: put the noodles in hot water and then add the little spice bag included in the packaging for flavour. There is a vegetarian version but that doesn't mean it's healthy. After all, it's just some dried noodles with a spice bag packed with lots of salt, E-numbers and additives. Far better to make your own soup! In this recipe I use the umami paste from the Weekends chapter (see page 15) as the base and I've added lots of fresh vegetables to make this a delicious and healthy soup.

Serves 2

100g noodles of choice
1 sweet potato, spiralised (alternatively, use
  a julienne cutter or make ribbons with a swivel-
  head peeler)
1 courgette, spiralised (see above)
vegetables of choice, such as sugarsnap
  peas, cooked broccoli, beansprouts, finely
  sliced pak choi, radish slices

sliced fresh chilli, to taste
2 teaspoons freshly grated ginger
2 tablespoons freshly chopped herbs such as
  coriander, chives or Thai basil
2 tablespoons Umami Paste (see page 15),
  or more if you wish

Cook the noodles according to the packet instructions; you want them al dente, not mushy. Drain and rinse the noodles, and divide them between two bowls or heatproof glass jars. Now add your vegetables to each portion, together with the chilli, ginger and herbs. Top each one with 1 tablespoon of the umami paste. Pour over 500ml of hot water (this will dissolve the umami paste) and your healthy cup of noodles is ready!

SUMMER TOMATO TART WITH AVOCADO HERBED CREAM

In the height of summer, whenever I'm in France, every Tuesday morning I go to the 'pick your own' garden in the next village to get the most beautiful and tasty varieties of tomatoes. The garden is closed on Sundays and Mondays, so I have to be quick on Tuesdays, otherwise all the fresh tomatoes will go and there won't be anything left to use to make this tart – it's the perfect thing to eat on a hot day!

Serves 4

for the tart
2 tablespoons ground chia seeds or linseeds
200g blanched almond flour
100g fine oat flakes
½ teaspoon salt
500g tomatoes (preferably different colors),
 sliced horizontally
coarse (smoked) sea salt

for the avocado cream
2 medium avocados, halved and stoned
2 garlic cloves, finely chopped
large bunch of basil or tarragon (or a mix),
 reserve some for garnish
1 tablespoon lemon juice
½ teaspoon red chilli, optional
salt, to taste

Preheat the oven to 200°C/gas mark 6 and line the base of a 22cm loose-bottomed cake tin or a 35 x 12cm rectangular one with baking paper.

Mix the chia seeds or linseeds with 60ml water and leave for 5 minutes so that the seeds absorb the water. They will form an egg-like consistency to bind the ingredients together.

Using a fork, combine the seeds with the almond flour, oat flakes and salt in a large bowl. Using your hands, form into a ball. Press the ball with into the lined cake tin, using your fingers to press the crust mixture onto the base and sides of the tin. The result should be even and not too thick. Transfer the tin to the oven and bake for 12–15 minutes until the crust is light golden brown and there is a small gap between the crust and the tin. Remove from the oven and leave to cool slightly.

Meanwhile, make the avocado herbed cream. Mix all the ingredients together in a food-processor or blender until smooth. Taste to see whether it needs more seasoning.

When your crust has cooled (it doesn't need long; 2 minutes is enough), spread the avocado cream evenly over the base then arrange the tomatoes, slightly overlapping, on top. Gently remove the tart from the tin and sprinkle over the coarse sea salt before serving with a green salad.

AUTUMN BOWLS WITH BALSAMIC REDUCTION

Using some roasted or cooked vegetables, cooked grains (done at the weekend) or leftovers from the days before, you can make these vegetable bowls as a super-quick weekday meal. This one is a fine example of a bowl that I like to make.

Serves 4

160g quinoa tricolore (or use 480g cooked
  grains)
1 teaspoon fennel seeds
4 ripe tomatoes (heirloom if you can find them),
  sliced in wedges
4 fresh figs, quartered
500g roasted pumpkin or cooked beetroots
  (see page 53)
bunch of fresh herbs, such as tarragon or basil,
  torn
salt and freshly ground black pepper

Cashew Mozzarella (see page 18) or 240g
  (drained weight) white beans, such as haricot,
  cannellini or butter beans, either home cooked
  or from a 400g jar/can (optional)

for the balsamic reduction
240ml balsamic vinegar
4 tablespoons maple syrup
sprigs of fresh thyme, washed

Unless you are using precooked quinoa (or another grain), cook it according to the instructions on the packet.

Meanwhile, make the balsamic reduction. Put the ingredients in a small pan and bring to a gentle boil. Leave to simmer for about 10–15 minutes to thicken. When the mixture is reduced by a third of its original volume, it's ready. Set aside to cool.

Dry-roast the fennel seeds in a dry non-stick or cast-iron pan over a low heat, moving the seeds around so that they don't burn. When they start to smell fragrant, which takes about 2 minutes, they are done. Remove the seeds from the pan and crush them using a pestle and mortar, a rolling pin or a spice grinder.

Tip the seeds into a medium bowl and add the tomatoes, figs, and salt and pepper to taste. Set aside.

Now you can assemble your autumn bowls. Start layering by adding some cooked quinoa to your bowl, then the cooked beetroots or roasted pumpkin. Continue by adding the prepared tomato-fig mixture to your bowls. If you are using the cashew mozzarella or beans, add them now. Scatter over the fresh herbs and serve drizzled with the balsamic reduction.

TIP:
This salad can easily be taken with you, in which case put the balsamic reduction in a separate container and pour it over just before eating.

CREAMY NO RECIPE PASTA

I could call this 'recipe' all sorts of things, but I won't. Let's just say it is a good and delicious pasta that hasn't got a real recipe. The base is always the same. With the addition of my cashew soured cream, you get a really lovely creamy pasta sauce. Furthermore, I add in whatever I have in my fridge, freezer or cupboard. Follow the basic recipe and use one of the add-ins that I suggest. When you are confident enough, just improvise and make this your own.

Serves 4

500ml Cashew Soured Cream, or its simple
  version (see page 17)
5 tablespoons nutritional yeast
juice of ½ lemon
3 garlic cloves, finely chopped
350–400g wholegrain pasta (or gluten-free
  pasta, if you prefer)
salt and freshly ground black pepper

Suggested add ins:
1 serving Slow-Roasted Cherry Tomatoes (see
  page 30) and 75g chopped rocket or spinach
200g defrosted peas or cooked broad beans,
  a small bunch of chopped fresh basil, flat-leaf
  parsley, tarragon or oregano and 1 tablespoon
  chopped fresh red chilli
1 head of cooked broccoli, divided into florets,
  zest of 1 lemon, 2 tablespoons toasted pine
  nuts and a dash of chilli powder, to taste
Roasted Pumpkin (see page 53), a good grating
  of nutmeg, 2 tablespoons freshly chopped flat-
  leaf parsley or sage and a dash of chilli
  powder, to taste
250g sautéed mushrooms of choice,
  1 tablespoon of mushroom powder (see
  page 15) and a small handful of chopped
  soft herbs, such as flat-leaf parsley, oregano
  or chives

Bring a large pan of water to the boil for the pasta.

Meanwhile, in a bowl, mix together the cashew soured cream, nutritional yeast, lemon juice, garlic and salt and pepper. Set aside.

When the water boils, cook the pasta according to the instructions on the packet. Before draining, reserve some of the cooking liquid.

Combine the drained pasta with the cashew soured cream and your chosen add-ins. If the sauce is too thick, stir in a bit of the served cooking liquid. Serve hot.

CARROT AND COURGETTE FRITTERS WITH ITALIAN SALSA VERDE

Making a vegetable the star of my meal is mostly what I do. Where traditional menus always focus on the meat, I focus on the greens. I use what I have in my home and what is in season. I always have carrots, because they are so versatile: you can eat them raw as a snack, make juice, use them in a stir fry, use them in soups or you can add them to a plant-based burger. Here I make carrots into fritters. They are not difficult to make and you can eat any leftovers as a quick snack, add them to a salad or serve them in a wrap the next day. I have paired the sweet flavour of the carrot with a flavoursome Italian salsa verde. *Buon appetito!*

Makes about 10

4 medium carrots, coarsely grated
1 medium courgette, coarsely grated
1 teaspoon salt
150g chickpea (gram) or wholegrain flour
good pinch of chilli powder
2 teaspoons dried thyme
zest of 1 lemon
3 tablespoons chopped flat-leaf parsley

for the salsa verde
large bunch flat-leaf parsley, coarsely chopped
juice of ½ lemon
1–2 garlic cloves, finely chopped
1 tablespoon chopped capers
1½ teaspoons Dijon mustard
2–3 tablespoons natural plant-based yogurt

Combine the grated carrots and courgettes with the salt and leave them in a colander for 5 minutes to release their water. Place them in a couple of sheets of kitchen paper and squeeze out the excess moisture.

Combine the flour, salt, chilli, thyme, lemon zest and parsley with 150ml water in a large bowl. Mix until there are no clumps. Add in the grated vegetables and coat them with the dough mixture.

Heat a non-stick pan over a medium heat, drop 2–3 tablespoons of the mixture into the pan and press it down to form a patty. Cook for 5–7 minutes on one side until the top starts to look dry and small bubbles appear. Then flip the patty and bake it for a further 5–7 minutes. Repeat until the whole mixture has been used.

While the fritters are cooking, make the salsa verde by combining all the ingredients in a small food-processor and pulse chopping them until they form a pesto-like consistency. Transfer the salsa verde to a small bowl.

When all the fritters are cooked, serve them with the salsa verde and some salad leaves such as watercress.

URAP-URAP WITH KECAP SAUCE AND SAMBAL

Part of Dutch culture is influenced by its former colony, Indonesia, and Indonesians who have settled in the Netherlands have enriched our food culture in ways we couldn't imagine before. Dishes such as *nasi*, *bami* and *saté* are now so famous in Holland that almost everyone eats them once a week. *Urap-urap* is less well known, but equally delicious. It is a traditional steamed vegetable salad with a spiced and grated coconut topping. There are a few components to this dish and you may think this is a lot of work, but in fact your kitchen equipment does most of it. Allow this dish to sweep you off your feet and leave your guests impressed!

Serves 4

300g wholegrain rice (for this dish I like the
   red variety)
400g French beans, trimmed and sliced into
   4–5cm pieces
300g cavolo nero, kale or savoy cabbage,
   central ribs removed and cut into bite-sized
   pieces
125g bean sprouts

for the sambal (hot chilli sauce)
100g fresh chillies, roughly chopped
2–3 garlic cloves, finely chopped
1 small red onion or shallot, diced
3cm piece of fresh ginger, peeled and chopped
juice of ½ lemon or 2 tablespoons raw apple
   cider vinegar
2 tablespoons shoyu or tamari sauce

for the kecap sauce
120ml shoyu or tamari sauce
120ml maple syrup
½ red chilli, sliced
2 star anise, whole
3 garlic cloves, crushed
3 slices of fresh ginger
1½ teaspoons cornflour or arrowroot blended
   with 1 tablespoon water

for the coconut topping
1 shallot, finely diced
4 garlic cloves, finely chopped
½ red chilli, deseeded and finely chopped, or
   1 teaspoon sambal (see left)
100g desiccated coconut (unsweetened)
1 teaspoon ground turmeric
1 teaspoon ground coriander
1 tablespoon maple syrup or coconut sugar
1 tablespoon shoyu or tamari sauce

Start by rinsing and cooking the rice according to the packet instructions.

Put all the ingredients for the sambal in a food-processor (you might want to wear disposable food gloves for handling these chillies) and pulse to a smooth sauce-like consistency. Transfer the sambal to a small jar or bowl and set aside.

To make the kecap sauce, put all the ingredients except the cornflour in a small pan over a low heat. Stir until it comes to a gentle boil and then lower the temperature so that it can reduce and thicken – about 10–15 minutes. When the sauce has thickened, stir in the blended cornflour. It will take less than a minute to thicken the sauce a little more. Pour the kecap into a small bowl and set aside.

continued ⟶

⟶ Next make the coconut topping by adding the shallot, garlic and chilli or sambal to a non-stick or cast-iron pan over a medium-high heat. Add a splash of water to water-fry the ingredients. When the shallot is soft and lightly golden, add the desiccated coconut, turmeric and coriander to the pan. The texture of this mixture should be more dry than liquid; like a crumble. Desiccated coconut will burn quickly, so stir often until it is golden brown. Add the maple syrup and shoyu sauce, give it a good stir and cook for a further minute, stirring continually.

While the topping cooks, steam the vegetables. Bring a large pan of water to the boil and set a steamer on top. Once it boils, add the French beans – they will need the longest time to cook.

After 5–6 minutes add the kale; this takes only 2–3 minutes. Add the beansprouts for the final minute of the cooking time – you don't want the vegetables to be overcooked, so keep an eye on them and taste to check whether they are ready. The beans should be cooked but still have a light crunch.

When the vegetables are ready, combine them with the coconut topping. Serve with the rice, the sambal and the kecap sauce. Enjoy your meal – or *selamat makan* as they say in Indonesia!

CHIA PUDDING FOR ALL SEASONS

This pudding is easy to make in advance and it lasts up to five days in the fridge. It is adaptable to every season if you use different fruit toppings. You can add different spices, too. On days when you are really hungry, you can add your favourite granola (see page 102) to make it even more fulfilling. A very versatile pudding indeed!

Makes about 1 litre/Serves 4

for the basic recipe
150g black or white chia seeds
1 litre nut milk or other plant-based milk
120ml your preferred liquid sweetener (maple
  or brown rice syrup or coconut nectar)

¾ teaspoon vanilla powder
pinch of good-quality salt

Put the chia seeds in a large bowl or container such as a mason jar. Stir in the milk, sweetener, vanilla powder and salt. Stir well or, if the container has a lid, close the lid and shake. It will take about 10–15 minutes for the chia seeds to soak up all the ingredients. Shake or stir every 5 minutes to ensure the seeds really absorb all the milk.

ADDITIONAL SPICES YOU CAN ADD TO THE BASIC RECIPE:

For a 'Golden Turmeric' pudding add:
2 teaspoons ground turmeric, 1 teaspoon ground ginger, 1 teaspoon ground cinnamon and a few grinds of black pepper

For a 'Chai' pudding add:
1 tablespoon carob or cacao powder,

1½ teaspoons ground cinnamon, ¾ teaspoon ground ginger, pinch of nutmeg and ½ teaspoon ground cardamom

For a 'Decadent' pudding add:
6 tablespoons carob or cacao powder

FRUIT COMBINATIONS TO USE AS A TOPPING FOR YOUR CHIA PUDDING:

• 250g stoned apricots, sliced or cubed, combined with 125g raspberries, 125g blueberries, handful of chopped unsalted pistachio nuts and 1 teaspoon orange blossom water (optional)
• 250g stoned plums, sliced, 125g blackberries, 1 pear, cubed or sliced, ½ teaspoon ground

cardamom and a handful of chopped walnuts
• 2 (blood) oranges, peeled and cut into slices or segments, 5 Medjool dates, stoned and sliced, the seeds of 1 pomegranate and ½ teaspoon ground cinnamon.

continued ⟶

——→ ADD THIS RHUBARB AND STRAWBERRY COMPOTE FOR A
SPRING VERSION OF CHIA PUDDING:

250g rhubarb, chopped into 3cm pieces
250g strawberries, hulled (reserve a few for
  decoration)
juice of 1 orange

60ml brown rice syrup
1½ teaspoons rosewater (optional)
1½ teaspoons cornflour or arrowroot, blended
  with 2 tablespoons water

Add all the ingredients except the cornflour to a pan and bring to the boil over a low-medium heat. Turn down the heat once the fruits start to release their juices and the liquid starts to bubble. Leave it to simmer for 5–7 minutes. Taste to check whether the compote needs additional sweetening. Stir in the blended cornflour so that the compote binds – this takes about a minute. Allow the compote to cool and store in the fridge. Serve this on top of your chia pudding.

TIP:
If you put the chia pudding and the fruits in a mason jar, you can easily take it to work with you.

NO TIME
AT ALL

There are no excuses not to eat healthy food even when you are in hurry, whether it's breakfast, lunch or dinner time. That doesn't mean that you just have to grab a snack either. In this chapter I will show you that within 15 minutes you can have a delicious and healthy meal. For breakfast you can try my granola or smoothie bowl, for lunch there's my chickpea shawarma and in the evening you can enjoy a classic meal like pasta, pizza or curry. It's all here!

SPEEDY CHEATS' NUT MILK

This speedy nut milk is the answer if you are out of cartons of plant-based milk. It calls for just three ingredients and a blender. Once you have tried the basic recipe, you can make it your own by adding other ingredients, such as vanilla, cinnamon, cacao or carob.

Makes 500ml

3 tablespoons nut butter (almond, cashew, peanut butter, etc.)

pinch of salt (only if you are using a pure nut butter, one without added salt)

Add your ingredients to a blender with 500ml water and blend until a 'milk' forms. Use immediately or within 24 hours.

SMOOTHIE BOWL

If you see all the Instagram pictures of smoothie bowls, you might think no one eats anything else. But perhaps these smoothie lovers are right. A smoothie makes a wonderful light breakfast and a great dessert, one that can be made in no time. All you need are frozen berries, a blender and your phone ready to take a nice picture and join the #smoothiebowl hashtag!

Serves 2–3

125g frozen raspberries

125g frozen strawberries

125g frozen blueberries (I like wild ones best)

3 bananas

150ml nut milk of choice

1 teaspoon lemon or lime juice

½ teaspoon vanilla powder

2 Medjool dates, stoned

to serve

fresh fruit of choice

chopped nuts of choice

Put the frozen berries, bananas, nut milk, lemon juice, vanilla powder and dates in a high-speed blender and blend until smooth. Pour into two or three bowls and serve with fresh fruit and chopped nuts.

BREAKFAST POLENTA (SWEET AND SAVOURY)

When the temperature outside drops below 12°C, there is only one breakfast I really start to crave: a wholesome bowl of soothing and warming porridge. All kinds of grains, including pseudograins like buckwheat and rolled grains, can be prepared as a porridge. This particular one is made from polenta. Use quick-cook polenta as it cooks in minutes (traditional polenta can take up to 40 minutes). So check the label before you buy it.

SWEET POLENTA PORRIDGE – Serves 2–3

85g quick-cook polenta
600ml almond milk (you can use the Speedy
  Cheats' Milk on page 98)
½ teaspoon vanilla powder
½ teaspoon allspice
½ teaspoon cinnamon, plus extra to serve
60ml maple or brown rice syrup

To serve
sliced fruits, such as pineapple, banana,
  mangoes or dates
coconut yogurt
chopped mint

Put the polenta and the almond milk in a pan and bring it to a boil, stirring with a whisk. When the polenta starts to boil and thicken, reduce the heat and add the vanilla, allspice, cinnamon and sweetener. Keep stirring from time to time and let it cook for 5–7 minutes. Pour into two to three bowls and serve with fruit, coconut yogurt, chopped mint and a sprinkle of cinnamon.

SAVOURY POLENTA – Serves 2–3

85g quick cook polenta
600ml almond milk
1 teaspoon dried oregano
1 tablespoon nutritional yeast
½ teaspoon salt
2 large handfuls finely cut greens, such as kale,
  Swiss chard or spring greens

250g fresh or Slow roasted Cherry Tomatoes
(see page 30)
small handful of soft herbs, such as basil,
  tarragon, parsley or chives
Savoury Toppings (see pages 24–25) or
  chopped nuts of your choice
chilli flakes

Put the polenta and the almond milk in a pan and bring it to a boil, stirring with a whisk. When the polenta starts to boil and thicken, reduce the heat and add the oregano, nutritional yeast and salt. Continue to stir from time to time for 3 minutes. Add the greens and cook for a further 2–3 minutes. Taste to see if it needs a bit more salt and adjust accordingly. Remove from the heat. Pour into two or three bowls and serve the tomatoes, chopped herbs, savoury topping or nuts and a touch of chilli.

STOVE-TOP GRANOLA

Did you ever get a packet of granola from a shop and look at the ingredients and the price? Well, I did. Call me Dutch, but if you make your own granola it is far less expensive, has no refined sugars, trans-fats or other questionable things and, best of all, you can put in the things that you love. And by cooking the granola in a pan on the hob, you can make it in minutes. So no excuses, this recipe will have you creating your own granola in no time. I am sure you are going to love making and eating it.

Makes 5 servings

150g rolled oats
50g sunflower seeds

50g pumpkin seeds
60ml maple syrup

Add the oats and seeds to a cast-iron or non-stick pan and place over a medium heat. You need to toast the ingredients, so stir frequently to prevent it from burning. The rolled oats should turn golden and fragrant and the seeds will start to pop. This will take about 6–8 minutes.

Remove from the heat and add the maple syrup to the hot pan. Stir quickly to coat all the ingredients in the syrup, then take the granola out of the pan and spread it on a sheet of baking paper to cool down. If you want to add some dried fruit (about 50g), this is the time.

Once cooled (this will take just 2 minutes or so) it's ready to eat. This granola is good served with some speedy cheats' nut milk (page 98), plant-based yogurt or some seasonal fruits (or a mix).

The granola will keep for 10–14 days in an airtight container.

INDIAN-STYLE TOFU SCRAMBLE WITH QUICK MANGO CHUTNEY

Most people who start eating a plant-based diet don't really understand tofu, finding it bland and lacking in flavour. I must admit that they are right, but, as with chicken or cauliflower, which are also bland-tasting, you have to add the flavours you love. Consider tofu as a vehicle for many different flavours. I am sure that the Indian spices in this dish, paired with the chutney, will change the mind of any 'tofu-doubter'.

Serves 2

½ teaspoon black mustard seeds

¼ teaspoon cumin seeds

¼ teaspoon coriander seeds

150g cherry tomatoes, quartered (you can also use cooked sweet potato or pumpkin chunks)

1 teaspoon curry powder

4 spring onions, chopped into 1cm pieces

250g medium-firm tofu, drained and mashed with a fork to the consistency of scrambled egg

2 handfuls of washed spinach (about 100g)

1 green chilli (deseeded if you like it less hot), sliced

salt (use kala namak, Indian black salt, if you can find it)

For the chutney (makes a large jar)

½ teaspoon cumin seeds

2 mangoes, halved and flesh cut off the stones in halves

thumb-sized piece of ginger, peeled and chopped

½ teaspoon red chilli powder (for less heat use ¼ teaspoon)

½ teaspoon ground cardamom

1 tablespoon raw apple cider vinegar

2 Medjool dates, stoned and chopped

½ red onion, chopped

salt

Start by making the chutney. Dry-roast the cumin seeds in a cast-iron pan – just 30 seconds over a low heat will do. When the seeds start to smell fragrant, they are done.

If you have a pestle and mortar grind the seeds and set aside. If not, it's fine to leave them whole.

Scoop the mango flesh off their skins and add it to the bowl of your blender along with the ground cumin, ginger, chilli, cardamom, vinegar, dates and onion, then blend until smooth. Taste and add salt to your liking. Set aside.

For the scramble, use the same pan to dry-roast the mustard, cumin and coriander seeds until fragrant. Add the cherry tomatoes, curry powder and onions and increase the heat to medium-high. If needed, add a splash of water. Fry for about 3 minutes until the onions and tomatoes have softened. Now add the tofu and spinach and mix well. It is ready when the spinach is wilted. Top with the green chilli and season with salt to taste.

Serve with the chutney, some flatbreads and onion pickle (see pages 27 and 42).

VEGAN PASTA PUTTANESCA

There are many stories surrounding the origin of this dish, largely due to its name, which some sources say refers to ladies of the night. But one thing is sure: this pasta is packed with flavour. It's salty because of the capers and olives, hot from the chilli and fragrant from the garlic. A real mix of great tastes!

Serves 4

400g pasta of your choice (spelt, wholegrain, gluten-free)

for the sauce
1 red onion, chopped
500g cherry tomatoes, quartered (or if you are in a real hurry use 300g Slow-roasted Cherry Tomatoes, see page 30)
5 garlic cloves, chopped

½ teaspoon (or more) chilli powder or chilli flakes
2 teaspoons drained capers, roughly chopped
75g good-quality black olives, such as Kalamata, drained and roughly chopped
salt (optional)

to serve
2 tablespoons washed flat-leaf parsley, chopped
nut parmesan (see page 26)

Bring a large pan of water to the boil for the pasta. Begin making the sauce by water-frying the onion in a large non-stick frying pan over a high heat. Start with no liquid and, when the pieces are caramelising, add a little water to deglaze the pan (if you use too much water the onion will cook and not fry). Fry the onion for 3–5 minutes until golden and soft. Add the tomatoes and garlic to the pan. Cook for about 2 minutes, then add the chilli, capers and olives. Reduce the heat to medium and continue to cook for a further 6–8 minutes, adding a little more water if needed to ensure the sauce doesn't burn. Taste before adding any salt (remember the olives and capers are very salty).

Meanwhile, cook the pasta according to the packet instructions and then drain, reserving some of the cooking water. Add the pasta to the sauce and, if needed, a splash of the cooking water to loosen it slightly. Serve with some chopped parsley and nut parmesan.

PASTA WITH COURGETTES, WHITE BEANS AND GRILLED LEMON

Pasta is one of those simple, fast meals and always a crowd pleaser. This summery pasta dish is a perfect example of lazy cooking with maximum results.

Serves 4

2 tablespoons pine nuts
2 lemons, halved
350–400g pasta of your choice (spelt, wholegrain, gluten-free)
220g (drained weight) cooked white beans, such as cannellini or haricot, homemade or from a 400g jar/can

2 courgettes (yellow, green or both), coarsely grated
1–2 garlic cloves finely chopped
3–4 tablespoons Cashew Soured Cream (see page 17) or natural plant-based yogurt
½ bunch of mint, leaves picked and chopped
salt and chilli flakes

Bring a large pan of water to the boil for the pasta. Dry-roast the pine nuts in a dry pan over a low heat until golden brown and set them aside.

Heat a ridged cast-iron or griddle pan and griddle the lemons, cut side down, until a grill pattern appears. Cook the pasta according to the packet instructions. Add the white beans into the pasta at the very last minute. Reserve some of the cooking liquid (a small cup will do) before draining the beans and the pasta. Return them to the same pan or a large bowl and add the grated courgette, garlic, cashew cream, salt and chilli to taste. Mix in some of the reserved cooking liquid to loosen it slightly. Serve the pasta with the fresh mint, grilled lemon and pine nuts.

PIZZA COMING UP!

Pizza, what's not to love about it? It is one of the most famous foods in the world, often sold frozen and ready made. When time is lacking, people tend to throw a ready-made pizza in the oven for a quick meal. They forget (sometimes deliberately) that it can be filled with fats, calories and salt. I think this meal can be so much better and with flatbreads you have an ideal pizza base. If you make flatbreads at the weekend and have some tomato sauce left, you are nearly there. You just need a topping. I use figs, mozzarella and rocket for the topping in this recipe. But don't be afraid to experiment and use whatever is in your fridge. The key to a great pizza? A hot oven and good-quality ingredients. You're never going back to ready-made pizza again!

Makes 2 pizzas

2 flatbreads, homemade (see page 27) or
  store bought (wholegrain)
1 serving of tomato sauce (see page 30) or from
  a jar (good quality)
3 fresh figs, cut into rounds

a couple of balls of homemade Cashew
  Mozzarella (see page 18), sliced
50g pine nuts
splash of good-quality balsamic vinegar
75g rocket

Preheat the oven to its highest setting.

On each flatbread, spread 3 tablespoons tomato sauce and top with the figs, mozzarella, pine nuts and a splash of good-quality balsamic vinegar.

If possible, place both pizzas in the middle of the hot oven; if not, cook them one at a time. Bake for about 4-5 minutes until the bottom is crispy.

Remove from the oven and scatter over some rocket for extra punch. Now eat.

MEXICAN BLACK BEAN SALAD WITH JALAPEÑO CREMA

Beans are one of the staple ingredients in my vegan kitchen – and for good reason. They are high in protein, minerals and fibre, low in fat and very cheap. They are a mainstay in many traditional food cultures. Think of Indian dahl, a daily meal for millions; stews and soups from Italy (people in Tuscany were often referred to as *mangiafagioli* or 'bean-eaters'); and the chillies and mashed refried beans of Mexico. In this Mexican-inspired dish, the beans are not mashed but treated as a crouton; the black beans have a crisp outside and are flavoured with Mexican spices.

Serves 4

for the salad
2 fresh corn on the cob, kernels cut off
1 Romaine or 2 small Little Gem lettuces,
  washed and leaves separated
250g various coloured tomatoes, sliced (or
  halved if you use tiny ones)
small bunch of fresh coriander, leaves picked
220g (drained weight) black beans from a 400g
  jar/can
1½ teaspoons paprika
½ teaspoon chilli powder
1½ teaspoons dried oregano
1 **teaspoon ground cumin**
½ teaspoon garlic granules
salt

for the jalapeño crema
250ml natural plant-based yogurt
1 avocado, stoned and peeled
1 jalapeño pepper, deseeded and sliced (or use
  1½–2 tablespoons pickled jalapeño)
juice of 1 lime
1 small garlic clove, chopped
salt

Start by cooking the corn kernels. Heat some water in a pan over a medium heat and add the kernels. Blanch for two minutes, then drain and set aside.

Now make the jalapeño crema. Add all ingredients to a blender (you can also use an immersion blender) and blend until smooth. Taste and add salt as required. Pour the crema into a bowl and set aside.

Arrange the salad leaves, tomatoes, corn kernels and coriander leaves on a large plate and set aside.

Put the beans and all the spices in a bowl and stir to coat the beans with the spices. Add salt to taste. Heat a dry pan over a medium-high heat and add the spicy beans. Quite soon the beans will become dry and start to break up or pop – this is fine. Shake the pan so that the beans don't burn. They should be heated through, but not overly hot. Scatter the beans on top of the salad and serve with the jalapeño crema.

SUPER-FAST THAI BLENDER CURRY

Thai food is the perfect cuisine for those moments when you need a tasty meal but time is short. Thai dishes are based on quick cooking techniques using fresh aromatic and spicy ingredients. By making a curry in a blender, you save time and still get a great meal that is super delicious and packed with goodness.

Serves 4

3 spring onions, chopped

1 thumb-sized piece of ginger, roughly chopped

juice of 1 lime

bunch of coriander, roughly chopped (reserve a few leaves for garnish)

3 garlic cloves, crushed

2 tablespoons coconut sugar

1½ tablespoons shoyu, tamari or Umami Paste (see page 15)

1 red or green chilli (more if you like it hot), plus extra to serve

400ml coconut milk

¼ cup vegetable stock (see page 14) or water

1 head of broccoli, cut into florets and the stem peeled and sliced, or 300g long-stem broccoli

1 courgette, sliced lengthways and cut into half moons

200g mangetout, halved

100g raw cashew nuts

2 limes, cut into wedges

salt

cooked wholegrain rice or noodles, to serve

Preheat the oven to 180°C/gas mark 4 and line a baking tray with baking paper.

To make the curry sauce, put the spring onions, ginger, lime juice, coriander, garlic, coconut sugar, shoyu, tamari or umami paste, chilli, coconut milk and stock or water into a blender. Blend until smooth. Transfer everything to a large pan and bring to the boil. Add the broccoli and courgette and cook for 4–5 minutes over a medium heat. Then add the mangetout. Cook for a further 3–4 minutes until the vegetables are done, but still have some bite – you don't want to overcook them. Taste to see whether it needs some salt and adjust accordingly.

Meawhile put the cashews on the lined tray and bake in the middle of the oven for 4 minutes. Stir the cashews and cook them for a further 3–5 minutes until golden. The nuts can burn easily, so check them frequently. When they are ready, remove from the oven and allow the cashews to cool a little, then roughly chop them.

Top the curry with the chopped cashews, wedges of lime, reserved coriander leaves and maybe some more chopped chilli for additional heat. Serve the curry with some cooked wholegrain rice or noodles.

ASIAN SALAD WITH TEMPEH MINCE

Tempeh is an Indonesian product made from fermented soy beans. Chopped finely or even grated it makes a wonderful alternative to beef mince – so good, in fact, that you can easily fool a big meat lover.

Serves 4

250g tempeh
250g noodles (mung bean or rice)
200g peas
handful of sugarsnap peas or mangetout, halved
1 teaspoon garlic granules
1 tablespoon maple syrup
3 tablespoons water
1 red chilli, deseeded and finely chopped
1 teaspoon five-spice
1 tablespoon rice vinegar or balsamic
4 tablespoons soy or tamari sauce
½ small Chinese cabbage, shredded

1 courgette, spiralised or cut with a julienne cutter
½ bunch of spring onions, finely chopped

for the sauce
4 tablespoons soy or tamari sauce
4 tablespoons water
1 tablespoon rice vinegar or balsamic
1 teaspoon freshly grated ginger
1 teaspoon maple syrup
1 tablespoon tahini
chilli flakes, to taste

Begin by chopping up your tempeh using a food processor until it has a crumbly consistency.

Bring a large pan of water to the boil for your noodles and cook according to the instructions on the packet. Add the peas and sugarsnaps to the boiling water at the very last minute of the cooking time. Rinse under the cold tap and drain.

While the noodles are cooking, start making your tempeh mince. Add the tempeh to a hot dry pan. Stir-fry the tempeh while adding the

garlic, maple syrup, water, chilli, five-spice, vinegar and soy or tamari sauce. Cook for about 4–5 minutes, adding a splash of water, if needed, to prevent it burning. Set aside.

Make the sauce by combining all the ingredients in a small bowl. Set aside. Tip the noodles into a large bowl or a plate. Mix the Chinese cabbage, peas, courgette and spring onions with the noodles. Add the tempeh mince and the sauce on top.

TIP:
For extra crunch, use the almond and sesame topping (see page 24).

JAPANESE-STYLE GRILLED AUBERGINES WITH SWEET AND SOUR CUCUMBER

As soon as August comes, I start looking forward to getting young fresh aubergines from a 'pick your own' near my home in France. They are grown in glasshouses and are quite hard to harvest since the stems have small spikes. Aubergines are often baked or grilled while drenched in oil, but instead of using a lot of oil, I prefer to steam the aubergines and then add flavourings to them. The umami paste from the Weekends chapter (see page 15) gives this dish a Japanese touch. The tart cucumber salad on the side is a good match.

Serves 4

For the aubergines
4 aubergines, halved
1 tablespoon Umami Paste (see page 15)
1½ teaspoons maple syrup
pinch of chilli flakes or powder
1 teaspoon freshly grated ginger
3 spring onions, sliced finely
3 tablespoons sesame seeds or Almond and Sesame Topping (see page 24)

For the cucumber salad
1 cucumber, sliced into ribbons
1 small shallot, finely sliced
2 tablespoons rice vinegar (or raw apple cider vinegar)
1 tablespoon maple syrup
1 teaspoon shoyu sauce
sea salt and freshly ground black pepper

To serve
cooked grains or noodles, to serve

Preheat your grill to the highest setting, bring a large pan of water to the boil and set a steamer on top.

Cut a criss-cross pattern on the cut face of the aubergines, but not so deep that you pierce the bottom. Steam the aubergines for 6–8 minutes until they are cooked. Remove from the steamer and, if necessary, set aside on some kitchen paper to drain any excess moisture.

Meanwhile, make the cucumber salad by mixing all the ingredients in a bowl. Taste and adjust the seasoning if necessary.

Mix the umami paste, 2½ tablespoons water, maple syrup, chilli and ginger in a small bowl. Brush the cut side of the aubergines with the mixture and place under the grill for 3–5 minutes until they are golden brown – keep an eye on them to check they don't burn.

Sprinkle the spring onions and sesame seeds or the topping on top of the aubergines. Serve with the cucumber salad and some cooked grains or noodles.

SUSHI BOWLS WITH WASABI PEAS

Ask my daughter what she wants to eat and one of the things she will shout out is: a sushi bowl. I couldn't agree more. I love to make sushi bowls – they're quick and easy and packed with flavour. When I prepare a meal with grains (for example quinoa or rice), I always prepare more than I need, so I can make a sushi bowl the next day. It's not very complicated at all and when you are pressed for time this is an excellent idea for a healthy meal.

Serves 4

200g uncooked quinoa (about 600g cooked)
300g frozen peas, defrosted
2–3 teaspoons wasabi paste (or 2 teaspoons powder mixed with 1½ teaspoons water)
½ teaspoon salt (or more to taste)
2 teaspoons sushi or brown rice vinegar
3 ripe avocados, halved and stoned
½ cucumber, finely sliced
handful of micro sprouts
75g baby gem lettuce, leaves separated
¼ red cabbage, finely shredded

1 sheet of nori, snipped finely with scissors
Red Onion Pickle (see page 42) or 4 tablespoons finely chopped spring onions
4 tablespoons Almond and Sesame Topping (see page 24) or dry-roasted sesame seeds

for the dressing
60ml soy sauce
1 tablespoon sushi or brown rice vinegar
1–2 teaspoons freshly grated ginger (optional)

Cook the quinoa according to the packet instructions (or use 600g leftover cooked quinoa or rice).

Make the wasabi peas by putting the defrosted peas, wasabi paste, salt, vinegar and the flesh of one avocado in the bowl of a food-processor. Pulse-chop the mixture until all is combined, but the peas are still crumbly – the texture doesn't have to be completely smooth. Taste and adjust the seasoning and set aside.

Remove the skin from the two remaining avocados and slice the flesh thinly.

Combine and stir the dressing ingredients with 2 tablespoons water in a small bowl and set aside.

Divide the quinoa between four bowls. Now you are going to group each component on top of the quinoa or rice: ensure you don't mix the ingredients. Put 2–3 tablespoons of the wasabi peas in each bowl. Then arrange the avocado and cucumber slices, sprouts, salad leaves, shredded cabbage, nori and onion pickle over the bowl. Sprinkle with the topping or sesame seeds and pour the dressing over the bowls. *Oishii!*

CHICKPEA SHAWARMA AND CUCUMBER TZATZIKI

It's been a while since I last walked the streets after a night out in search for something to eat, but I am pretty sure that shawarma bread is still a favourite late-night snack (at least in Holland it is). The dish originates from the Levantine kitchen and it's still a very popular streetfood on the Arabian peninsula and beyond. What makes this dish so attractive? To my mind, shawarma is all about the spices and the sauce. With this recipe you can rustle up a quick and lovely shawarma, one so good that you'll want to run home to make it after a good night out rather than searching for a late night food place.

Serves 4

2 tomatoes, chopped

1–1½ tablespoons shawarma spice (see below) or baharat spice mix

440g chickpeas (drained weight), homemade or from two 420g jars/cans

salt to taste

wholegrain pitta breads, to serve

for the shawarma spice mix

2 teaspoons ground cumin

2 teaspoons ground cinnamon

2 teaspoons sweet paprika

2 teaspoons black pepper

1 teaspoon chilli powder

½ teaspoon ground turmeric

2 teaspoons garlic powder

1 teaspoon allspice

for the tzatziki

1 cucumber, deseeded and grated

2–3 garlic cloves

1 teaspoon lemon juice

120ml natural plant-based yogurt (or use the Cashew Soured Cream, see page 17)

good pinch of salt

3 tablespoons chopped dill or mint (optional)

First make the shawarma by simply combining all the spices together.

Cook the chopped tomatoes in a hot dry pan. After 1–2 minutes, add the spices and the chickpeas. Stir frequently to prevent burning. If necessary add a splash of water. Keep cooking until the chickpeas are hot – this takes about 5 minutes.

Meanwhile, make the tzatziki by combining the ingredients in a bowl and season to taste.

Serve the chickpea shawarma with wholegrain pitta breads or cooked grains topped with some tzatziki. You can also serve tahini sauce, some lettuce, pickles (see page 42), olives and maybe some smoky paprika hummus (opposite) to make a real festive Middle Eastern meal.

> **TIP:**
> The shawarma spice mix here will make a bit more than you need. Just store it in a small container and you will be prepared for your next use.

HARISSA AND GRILLED PAPRIKA HUMMUS

If there is one prepared dish that is always in my fridge it is hummus. I have jars of cooked chickpeas in my cellar, ready to make hummus and, of course, for the chickpea liquid (aquafaba) from the jar that I use as an egg substitute in many vegan dishes. I serve hummus on bread, as a dip for raw vegetables, as part of a mezze, as a sauce for whole roasted vegetables or even stirred into a pasta dish. The possibilities are endless, which makes it a firm family favourite. This recipe makes quite a large amount and is intended to be eaten as a main dish. Hopefully, it will provide some leftovers for the following day, but I can't promise that.

Makes 1 litre hummus

1½ teaspoons cumin seeds

440g (drained weight) chickpeas, homemade or from two 420g jars/cans (reserve 2 tablespoons for garnish)

2 grilled red peppers or prepared ones from a 295g jar (drained weight 185g; ensure they are sugar-free)

2 generous tablespoons of tahini

3–5 garlic cloves, chopped

1½ tablespoons harissa paste

salt

To serve

2 tablespoons sesame seeds (white, black or both)

handful of fresh soft herbs, such as mint, dill or coriander

Flatbreads (see page 27) or pitta bread

Pickles (see page 42)

raw vegetables, such as multi-coloured carrots and beetroots, cucumber, pepper, crisp salad leaves, tomatoes, radishes, etc.

Dry-roast the cumin seeds in a dry frying pan until fragrant. This won't take long, normally a minute or less, so stay with the seeds and stir often. Remove the seeds from the pan.

Put the cumin seeds and all the other ingredients for the hummus in a food-processor or blender with 200ml water and and blend until smooth.

Transfer the hummus to a large bowl and top with the sesame seeds, fresh herbs and the reserved whole chickpeas. Serve with the bread, pickles and raw vegetables.

OYSTER MUSHROOM BURGERS WITH GRILLED PAPRIKA MAYONNAISE

If there is one thing that's clear to me, I am never going to eat a 'real' burger again. And who needs one anyway? Plant-based burgers are full of flavours, far more interesting and so much better for you (and the environment) than meat-based ones. Of course, you can make a burger from beans and grains, but for a quick fix I choose meaty oyster mushrooms on a bun.

Serves 4

450g oyster mushrooms
4 wholegrain buns, halved
salad leaves
2 tomatoes, sliced
1 avocado, halved, stoned and sliced
Red Onion Pickle (see page 42) or red onion slices

For the grilled paprika mayonnaise
400g silken tofu or 500ml Cashew Soured Cream (see page 17)

grilled peppers from a 295g jar (drained weight 185g); ensure they are sugar-free
½ teaspoon fennel seeds
½ teaspoon smoked paprika
¼ teaspoon salt (use kala namak, Indian black salt, for a more egg-like taste)
1 tablespoon raw apple cider vinegar
1 tablespoon apricot jam (ensure it is sugar-free)

Preheat a griddle pan or panini maker. When the pan is very hot, add the mushrooms. Leave them for about 2–4 minutes before turning. (You might want to press down on the mushrooms with a spatula or even place a small heavy pan on top of the mushrooms – ensure the base is clean. Pressing down on the mushrooms makes them go all crispy.) If you wish, warm the buns on the grill too, cut-side down, until griddle marks appear.

While the mushrooms are cooking make the mayonnaise. Place all the ingredients in a blender and blend until smooth. Transfer the mayonnaise to a bowl.

When your mushrooms are cooked, assemble your burgers. Place a little salad on the bottom halves of the buns, then the tomatoes, mushrooms, avocado slices, the pickle or onion, and finally the mayonnaise. Close with the top halves of the buns. Ready!

CUCUMBER SOUP

When it's warm outside, I often don't feel like making difficult foods and start to prepare light and fresh dishes, like a cold soup. There are different chilled soups that have their origin in warmer climes – think of Spanish gazpacho, French vichyssoise, Russian borscht and Korean *naengguk*. In this recipe a main ingredient is cucumber, which is super-hydrating for the body and gives this soup its fresh and cooling effect, as does the melon. That is what I look for in the height of summer.

Makes 1.5 litres/Serves 4–6 as a starter

2 cucumbers, roughly chopped
3 spring onions
small bunch of mint, chopped
small bunch of dill, chopped
2 garlic cloves, finely chopped
juice of 1 lemon
1 teaspoon salt
good pinch of chilli powder
250ml plant-based milk
1 avocado, stoned and peeled

For the topping
¼ cantaloupe or honeydew melon, deseeded
cucumber ribbons, made with a potato peeler
1 teaspoon black sesame or nigella seeds
1 teaspoon cracked pink peppercorns or chilli
  flakes
dill sprigs

Start by scooping out some balls from your melon. Use a round melon baller or a small measuring spoon (a teaspoon is a good size). If you don't have this equipment, just cut your melon into cubes of about 2–3cm. Set the balls aside, together with all the other topping ingredients for your soup.

Add all the soup ingredients to your blender and blend until smooth (you may need to do this in two batches if your blender is small). Taste to

check whether it needs a bit more salt or chilli. The soup should be refreshing, so don't go overboard on the chilli. Divide the soup between four to six bowls and add the toppings to each individual bowl.

TIP:
This soup can easily be made in advance. Leave the soup to chill in the fridge for a couple of hours.

NINA'S LENTIL CHILLI

Sometimes you eat such a delicious dish that the recipe becomes a part of your repertoire. This was the case with one from Nina Olsson's book *Bowls of Goodness*. The original name of her recipe is 'loyal lentil chilli'. Since I first tried it, I have now cooked her lentil chilli so many times while adjusting it here and there. I am sharing my version of her recipe here.

Serves 4

3 spring onions, sliced into 1cm pieces
4 garlic cloves, finely chopped
3cm piece of ginger, grated
1 teaspoon cinnamon powder
1½ tablespoons garam masala
1 teaspoon cumin seeds
1 teaspoon smoked paprika
1 teaspoon ground turmeric
400g chopped tomatoes (fresh or canned)
240g (drained weight) cooked lentils, homemade (see page 32) or from a 400g jar or can

400ml coconut milk
2 medium sweet potatoes, peeled and coarsely grated
2 teaspoons Umami Paste (see page 15)
2 teaspoons hot sauce (try my Sambal, see page 90)
1 tablespoon maple syrup
200g greens, such as spinach or kale
salt or shoyu, to taste

Sweat the spring onions with a splash of water in a large non-stick pan. Once softened add in the garlic, ginger, cinnamon, garam masala, cumin, paprika and turmeric. Stir and, if needed, add a splash of water. When the onions are coated in the spices, add the chopped tomatoes, lentils, coconut milk, grated sweet potato, umami paste, hot sauce and maple syrup. Stir well, bring to the boil, then leave to simmer for 10 minutes. Then add in the greens and leave to wilt for a further 1–2 minutes. Taste to check whether it needs additional salt, or use a dash of shoyu, and it is ready to serve.

TIP:
Serve the chilli with some cooked grains, such as quinoa, or flatbreads, pickles (see page 42) and a dollop of Cashew Soured Cream (see page 17) or plant-based natural yogurt.

GREEK-INSPIRED BUTTER BEAN STEW

When I lived in Amsterdam, my husband and I often went out to dinner with my parents. One of my favourites was a family-owned Greek restaurant. I really loved how their focus was always on good fresh food. The Greek kitchen relies on fresh ingredients in dishes that are not complicated to make. Fresh herbs, such as oregano, mint, bay leaves, dill, parsley, basil, fennel seeds and thyme, are a prominent feature. This recipe, which is based on the popular *gigandes plaki* (giant beans), makes use of these typical Greek herbs. They turn a simple weekday meal into a quick holiday to Greece.

Serves 3–4

1 medium courgette, quartered lengthways
  and sliced
3–4 garlic cloves
2 teaspoons dried oregano (or 1½ tablespoons
  fresh, chopped)
¾ teaspoon ground cinnamon
1 teaspoon fennel seeds
400g chopped tomatoes, fresh or canned

240g (drained weight) butterbeans, homemade
  or from a 400g jar/can
1 bay leaf
300g bulgur wheat
salt and freshly ground black pepper
2 tablespoons fresh dill or flat-leaf parsley,
  to serve

Put the courgette and the garlic in a pan over a medium heat. Add 2–3 tablespoons water and sauté for 1–2 minutes. Stir in the oregano, cinnamon and fennel seeds. Then add the chopped tomatoes, butterbeans and bay leaf and bring to the boil. Leave to simmer for 8–12 minutes over a low-medium heat.

Meanwhile, cook the bulgur wheat following the instructions on the packet.

Once the stew and the bulgur wheat are cooked, season to taste, scatter over some of the fresh herbs and serve hot.

TIP:

For a more extensive meal, add tzatziki (see page 118), a tomato salad and some Kalamata olives. You can also serve the stew with the vegan feta from my previous book *Vegan in 7*.

NEW POTATO SALAD WITH RADISHES AND PEAS

Over the past few years it has seemed that the potato has become less popular as a staple in comparison with more exotic options like rice or noodles. In Holland the potato was once an essential everyday ingredient. Cooked potatoes were served almost every day with another vegetable (like cauliflower) and a piece of meat at six o'clock precisely. In my home we mashed the two vegetables together on our plate and poured the gravy from the meat over the top. In the old days, if you were very poor you ate only potatoes. Take a look at Vincent van Gogh's famous painting 'The Potato Eaters'. Also one of the most famous varieties of potatoes – 'Bintje' – comes from The Netherlands. Nowadays people no longer see the beauty of this ingredient, which is a shame. The potato is nourishing and gentle on the digestive system. The arrival of new potatoes always excites me and the recipe for this salad is a beautiful example of how good a potato can be.

Serves 4 as a main, 6 as a starter

750g baby potatoes, halved (larger ones quartered)
250g peas, defrosted if frozen
300ml natural plant-based yogurt or Cashew Soured Cream (see page 17)
2 teaspoons mustard, such as Dijon
1 tablespoon raw apple cider vinegar or lemon juice

small bunch of chives, finely chopped
small bunch of flat-leaf parsley, finely chopped
1–2 garlic cloves, finely chopped (optional)
small bunch of radishes, sliced
salt and pepper

Put the potatoes in a pan, cover with cold water and bring to the boil. Cook the potatoes until they are just done, but not overcooked – about 5–7 minutes. The potatoes are done if they can be easily pierced with a sharp-pointed knife. In the last minute of cooking time add the peas. Drain the potatoes and peas in a colander and set them aside while making the sauce for your potato salad.

In a large bowl combine the yogurt or cashew cream, mustard, vinegar or lemon juice, herbs and garlic and add salt and pepper to taste. Tip in the potatoes, peas and radishes. Gently combine everything until all the potatoes are covered with sauce. Mix gently – you don't want to break up the potatoes too much. Serve immediately or place in the fridge until ready to serve.

TIP:
This salad is good served with pickled onions (see page 42) on the side.

GREEN PUDDING FOR ONE

During the year, I usually go through different phases of what I like for breakfast. In winter it is generally porridge, then, when I have had enough, I switch to granola. When spring and finally summer comes, I crave fresh fruits. This pudding is an example of what I eat regularly once weather improves and the sun begins to shine.

Serves 1

2 medium bananas, peeled and cut into chunks
1 avocado, halved, stoned and peeled
zest and juice from 1 organic lime
2 tablespoons maple syrup
handful of spinach, washed

for the topping
1 green apple, quartered, cored and sliced
1 kiwi fruit, peeled and sliced
blueberries or blackberries

Put the bananas, avocado, lime zest and juice, maple syrup and spinach into a blender and mix until smooth. Taste to check whether it needs more sweetening and adjust to your taste. Put the mixture into a pretty bowl, add the toppings and devour.

> TIP:
> It's easy to make this simple pudding for more than one serving – just multiply the ingredients by the number of people. If you freeze this pudding it turns into a delicious ice cream.

SWEET CELEBRATIONS

Celebrations are often associated with sweets. For a birthday or a wedding you eat cake or tart; for other festive events in the calendar, such as Christmas or Easter, you may have a nice dessert. For less special occasions we still enjoy something sweet: a biscuit with our tea, or a muffin or bun for a quick snack. Most of the treats you can buy are overly processed, unhealthy and contain lots of sugar, milk and butter. So I make my own vegan ones that do not contain any refined sugars, milk or butter. As I explained in the introduction, a high speed blender is a great tool for making super smooth vegan creams. This chapter includes a super-light chocolate mousse and various cakes, tarts, cookies and muffins that are delicious and healthy at the same time, so you can indulge in a sweet treat on regular or special occasions.

AQUAFABA CHOCOLATE MOUSSE

There is a lot of talk about aquafaba. It may sound like an exotic ingredient, but in fact aquafaba means 'bean water' and it is the more appealing name for the thick liquid that forms after cooking certain pulses, such as white beans or chickpeas. Aquafaba is usually rinsed off the beans and discarded. However, it is a precious ingredient for the vegan cook, because it can be used as an egg substitute for baking, giving dishes an airy and eggy texture (3 tablespoons aquafaba equals 1 egg). When whipped up, aquafaba develops a meringue-like consistency. My light-as-air chocolate mousse is a perfect example of how good this egg substitute is.

Serves 4

120ml aquafaba, chilled
2 tablespoons maple syrup
120g vegan chocolate, preferably 70% cocoa
  solids and sweetened with coconut sugar

½ teaspoon vanilla powder
pinch of salt

Pour the aquafaba into the clean bowl of a stand mixer (or use a hand-held mixer) and beat for about 4–6 minutes until stiff white peaks form. Add the maple syrup to the mixture and gently fold it in using a metal spoon.

Roughly chop the chocolate, add to a separate heatproof bowl and place over a pan of simmering water, ensuring that the water is not in contact with the base of the bowl. Add the vanilla powder and salt to the melting chocolate and mix through. When the chocolate has melted, remove the bowl from the heat and leave it to cool for a minute.

Gently fold the cooled chocolate mixture into the whipped aquafaba using a spatula. Divide the chocolate mouse between four small bowls or glasses and place in the fridge for at least an hour.

You can serve the mousse as it is or top with berries, a dusting of ground cinnamon, cacao nibs or even a small amount of chilli flakes.

FROZEN BANANA LOLLIES

At the height of summer when the weather is too hot for anything, a refreshing ice cream comes to the rescue. So you run to the shop to get one. But, for me, even the ones labelled vegan are not very appealing. Shopbought ice cream is full of sugars, such as corn syrup, refined sugar or sugar syrup, so I prefer to make my own ice cream on a stick, using bananas and nuts.

Makes 12

6 medium bananas (ensure they are ripe
  but firm)
200g creamed coconut or coconut butter
200g raw cashews, soaked overnight and
  drained
180ml nut milk
½ teaspoon vanilla powder

80ml maple syrup
pinch of salt
60g blueberries, defrosted if frozen (I prefer wild
  blueberries if you can get them)
2½ tablespoons cacao or carob powder

you also need 12 wooden ice cream sticks

Peel then halve your bananas across the width. Gently insert a wooden stick vertically into the middle of each piece until it's about halfway through. Lay them on a tray lined with baking paper and freeze them for 2–3 hours until firm.

Meanwhile, make the outer layer. Bring some water to a simmer in a small pan and place the creamed coconut or coconut butter, in its original packaging (either plastic or a glass jar), into the water until it becomes liquid. Measure off 200g into the bowl of a high-speed blender.

Add the soaked cashews, nut milk, vanilla powder, maple syrup and salt to the liquid creamed coconut and blend until the mixture is very smooth.

Pour half the mixture into a bowl and set aside. Add the defrosted blueberries to the remaining

mixture in the blender and blend well. Pour the blueberry mixture into a glass.

Return the other half of the mixture back into the blender, add the cacao or carob powder and blend until mixed. Pour this into a second glass.

Take the frozen bananas out of the freezer and dip six of them into the blueberry cashew mixture. Shake off the excess mixture. Make sure each one is coated and place them back on the lined tray. Now dip the remaining six into the other mixture and shake off the excess as before. Place them on the baking tray and return the bananas to the freezer for at least 3 hours to freeze the coating. Enjoy them straight from the freezer.

CRÈME BRULÉE AUX MARRONS

You may think that chestnuts are a typical Christmas ingredient, but for me they are not. The official hunt for chestnuts in our family begins in Holland, in the first or second week of October. However the most beautiful and tastiest ones grow in France, in the Ardèche region, where they are protected as carefully as the French wine. Chestnuts from the Ardèche have their own *appellation d'origine protégée* (AOP), a certification of their quality and source. The French are rightly proud of their regional produce and Ardèche chestnuts are used in a variety of products. One of them is the crème de marrons, a sweet chestnut paste made with vanilla and sugar. It has a beautiful caramel-like taste and is often eaten on pancakes or added to cakes and tarts. In this recipe I combine my own crème de marrons with another famous French dessert: crème brulée.

Serves 4-6

100g raw cashews, soaked overnight and drained
300g unsweetened cooked chestnuts, crumbled
1 teaspoon vanilla powder
100ml maple syrup
220ml plant-based milk (I use almond milk)

pinch of salt
120ml aquafaba (see page 135), chilled for at least 3 hours

For the topping
4-6 tablespoons coconut sugar

To make the chestnut paste, put the soaked cashews into a high-speed blender together with the crumbled chestnuts, vanilla, maple syrup, milk and salt. Blend until very smooth. You might want to use the tamper and push down the mass from time to time to get a really soft creamy result. Set aside.

Pour the aquafaba into the bowl of a stand mixer (or use a hand-held mixer) and beat for 4-6 minutes until stiff white peaks form. Add the chestnut paste and blend briefly until combined. Scoop the chestnut mousse into four or six ovenproof ramekins. Place the ramekins in the fridge for 1-2 hours to firm up.

Preheat the grill to high. Spoon 1 tablespoon of coconut sugar over each chestnut mousse. Shake the ramekins back and forth to ensure you have an even layer. Place the ramekins under the grill and allow the sugar to caramelise. This will take around 5 minutes, but keep your eye on them: you don't want the coconut sugar to burn. Rotate the ramekins frequently to make sure the topping grills evenly. Remove the ramekins and leave them to cool a little. You can either serve them warm or put them back in the fridge to serve chilled – but note that, if you leave them in the fridge for too long, the topping may turn to caramel.

TIPS:

Add 3 tablespoons of cocoa (or carob) powder to the chestnut mousse to make a 'crème de marrons et du chocolat'.

Alternatively, skip the coconut sugar layer and serve this as a chilled mousse topped with some seasonal fruits, such as pomegranate seeds, clementine segments or physalis (cape gooseberries).

OVEN-ROASTED FIGS, GRAPES AND PEARS WITH ICE CREAM

In summer we all want to eat more raw fruits, crisp vegetables and fresh salads and use cooking methods that are not overly complicated to keep the produce light and fresh. Come autumn, my focus is on bringing gentle heat to my dishes. This means using warming spices, such as cinnamon, and turning on the oven, even for fruit desserts. Baked fruit becomes sweeter and softer and the flavour is changed and intensified – as this simple recipe shows.

Serves 4-6

4 ripe but firm pears, peeled
8 figs, quartered
250g red grapes
250g blackberries (defrosted if frozen)
1 bay leaf
1 cinnamon stick
100ml apple, grape or orange juice

for the ice cream
5 ripe bananas, sliced then frozen for at least 6 hours
1 teaspoon vanilla powder
60ml plant-based milk (coconut is good)
a few drops of liquid stevia (optional)

Preheat the oven to 200°C/gas mark 6. Quarter the pears, remove the cores, then slice each quarter into halves or thirds. The size should be roughly the same as the quartered figs. Put all the fruits into a shallow heatproof dish with the bay leaf, cinnamon and fruit juice. Bake for 20-25 minutes until the fruits have become sticky and the juices start to bubble. Remove the dish from the oven while you make the ice cream.

Put the frozen bananas in a high-speed blender with the vanilla, milk and stevia (if using). Whizz until smooth, using a tamper to push the bananas down. (You will have to use a high speed blender otherwise you risk damaging the motor of an ordinary blender. You can also use a food-processor, scraping down the sides from time to time.) The bananas will be grainy at first, but keep going and the texture will become softer. Keep an eye on the texture you want it to reach a soft-serve consistency, not become soupy or too liquid.

When you're happy with the texture, pour the mixture into a container and freeze for 30 minutes. Serve with the roasted fruits.

TIPS:
Use ripe, spotted bananas for the ice cream, because they will be sweetest. You can also make the ice cream in advance and freeze until needed. Any leftovers can be served the following day on porridge or pancakes.

When you don't feel like making ice cream, serve the roasted fruits with coconut yogurt or Cashew Soured Cream (see page 17).

GRILLED PEACHES WITH GINGER CREAM AND WALNUT PRALINE

The perfectly ripe peach is a tricky one to find. Most peaches are too hard when you buy them and, if you take them home to ripen, it is difficult to keep track of when they are soft, scented and sweet. Not to discourage you, no, not at all! For this recipe you can use peaches that are not perfectly ripe. You need a ridged griddle pan or panini maker.

Serves 4

350ml Cashew Soured Cream (see page 17)
  or coconut yogurt
2 teaspoons grated fresh ginger
1½ teaspoons ground cinnamon
½ teaspoon fresh grated nutmeg (optional)
½ teaspoon vanilla powder
pinch of salt

60ml maple or brown rice syrup
6 ripe but firm peaches, halved and stoned

For the praline
100g walnuts
2 tablespoons maple syrup
pinch of salt

In a bowl combine the cashew soured cream or coconut yogurt with the fresh ginger, cinnamon, nutmeg (if using), vanilla and salt. Set aside. (You can do this in advance, in which case put the mixture in the fridge.)

Dry roast the walnuts in a dry non-stick or cast-iron pan over a medium heat until golden brown. Stir frequently and after 3–4 minutes add the maple syrup and salt, stirring to coat all the nuts. Leave to cook for a further minute. Tip the walnuts out of the pan and spread them on baking paper to cool. Once the walnuts are cool, chop them roughly.

Now set your griddle pan or panini maker on high. The pan must be really hot before you start to grill the peaches. Lay the peaches cut side down on the pan and grill for about 3 minutes or until grill marks appear. Serve the peaches with the soured cream, maple or brown rice syrup and walnut praline.

TIP:
For a festive flourish, use some fresh lemon verbena or mint leaves or dried lavender flowers as an extra topping.

BANANA AND TOFFEE PARFAIT

'Cake in a glass' is the only way to describe this delightful parfait. It is based on the very popular banana and toffee pie, also known as 'banoffee pie'. Traditionally it is made with a sugar caramel and dairy cream. In this recipe I use Medjool dates for the caramel and cashew cream as a dairy substitute. What's not to love about this healthy take on a classic?

Serves 4

3 firm but ripe bananas, peeled and sliced

For the base
150g (about 8) Medjool dates, stoned
100g raw walnuts
2 tablespoons carob or cacao powder
pinch of salt

For the date caramel
150g (about 8) Medjool dates, stoned
80ml peanut butter (almond butter or tahini also work)

¼ teaspoon vanilla powder
good pinch of salt

For the cream
300ml Cashew Soured Cream (see page 17) or coconut yogurt
2 tablespoons maple or brown rice syrup
¼ teaspoon vanilla powder

Put all the ingredients for the base in a food-processor and whizz until the mixture resembles a crumble. Set aside.

To make the date caramel, put the dates, peanut butter, vanilla, salt and 180ml water in a blender. Blend until smooth, adding a splash more water if the texture is a bit too dense, until you reach desired consistency. Transfer the caramel to a bowl and set aside.

To make the cream layer, combine the cashew soured cream or coconut yogurt with the maple syrup and vanilla in a separate bowl and stir until mixed.

The parfaits are now ready to be assembled. Take four glasses and spoon in 2–3 tablespoons of the base mixture, then add 2–3 tablespoons of the caramel, then a couple of banana slices and top with the cream layer. Repeat the layers if any remains and you have space in your glass, or finish by adding a couple of sliced bananas on top of your cream layer.

Serve immediately or make ahead and chill in the fridge.

RASPBERRY AND COCONUT CHEESECAKE

This cheesecake has been a part of my repertoire for many, many years. It's an easy recipe and once you have made it a couple of times, I am sure it will be one of your favourites, too. Here I use raspberries, but all kinds of berries work well in this recipe, as do other fruits, such as mango, kiwi, persimmon or pineapple. I have tried all of these and they are equally delicious.

Serves 12

For the crust
150g blanched almond flour
100g fine oat flakes
3 tablespoons nut butter
3–4 tablespoons maple or brown rice syrup
pinch of salt

For the filling
1 litre coconut milk
1 teaspoon vanilla powder
120ml maple syrup

juice of ½ lemon
1 tablespoon nutritional yeast (optional)
1 tablespoon agar agar
3 tablespoons cornflour or arrowroot, combined
  with 3 tablespoons water

For the raspberry layer
500g raspberries (defrosted if frozen)
180ml apple juice
3 tablespoons cornflour (or arrowroot) combined
  with 3 tablespoons water

Preheat the oven to 180°C/gas mark 4 and line a 22cm loose-bottomed cake tin with baking paper.

Mix together the crust ingredients with a fork to create a crumbly texture. Then, with moist hands, form into a ball and firmly press into the base of the tin in an even layer. Bake for 12–15 minutes until the crust is slightly golden brown. Then remove the tin from the oven and leave it to cool while you make the filling.

Add the coconut milk, vanilla, maple syrup, lemon juice, nutritional yeast (if using) and agar agar to a pan and set over a low heat. Bring to a gentle boil while stirring constantly with a whisk. It is important to keep whisking at this stage, otherwise the agar agar will form into clumps, which you want to avoid. Cook for about 6 minutes. While continuing to stir, add

the arrowroot/cornflour mixture. It will thicken quickly – it takes about 1 minute. Pour this mixture into the tin, over the baked crust. Leave it to cool. It will take 2–3 hours for the coconut layer to become firm. Once the initial heat has gone, you can transfer the cake to the fridge to cool further.

When the coconut layer has firmed up completely, make the raspberry topping. Put the raspberries in a bowl and set aside. Pour the apple juice into a small pan and bring to a light boil. Stir the cornflour or arrowroot mixture before adding it to the apple juice. Whisk briskly until it thickens, then pour this mixture over the raspberries and gently stir to coat. Carefully pour on top of the coconut cheesecake to form an even layer. Allow to cool completely so the raspberry layer can set. Eat when ready or store in the fridge for up to 2 days.

APRICOT CLAFOUTIS

Clafoutis is a French baked dessert, like a flan made with batter and cherries. You can make it with other stone fruits such as plums, peaches or apricots, although purists will tell you that if you use anything other than cherries it isn't a clafoutis and it should be called a *flaugnarde*. In this recipe I have used apricots, and the batter is a vegan version instead of the traditional milk, eggs and flour one, but I'm sticking with the name clafoutis. The recipe is not complicated at all and it can be eaten warm or chilled and, if you like, served with some Cashew Soured Cream (see page 17) or coconut yogurt.

Serves 6

500g ripe but firm apricots, halved and stoned
35g cornflour
325ml almond milk (or other plant-based milk)
80g almond flour

3 tablespoons apple sauce (sugar-free)
80ml maple or brown rice syrup
¼ teaspoon vanilla powder

Preheat the oven to 200°C/gas mark 6. Arrange the apricots, cut side up, in a ceramic ovenproof dish.

Mix the cornflour with 3 tablespoons of the almond milk until dissolved, then add this to a large bowl along with the remaining ingredients and the rest of the almond milk.

Mix until no clumps remain and then pour the batter over the apricots.

Place the dish in the oven and cook for about 35 minutes until the batter is bubbly, golden and set in the centre. Remove from the oven and leave for at least 30 minutes before serving.

RAW MANGO MOUSSE MINI CAKES

For a long time I was on a raw food diet. During that period I ate no cooked meals, everything had to be raw, which means nothing was heated above 42°C. The idea is that by not heating your food the micronutrients stay alive and can contribute to better health. With this diet came new ideas and innovative techniques for making cakes, mousses and creams with nuts. Although I no longer eat a raw food diet full time, I still use these techniques. These delicious mini cakes are one example.

Makes 12

For the crust
80g desiccated coconut, unsweetened
80g almonds
8 Medjool dates, stoned

For the filling
200g creamed coconut, packet unopened
150g dried mango, soaked overnight
200g raw cashew nuts, soaked overnight

½ teaspoon vanilla powder
juice of 2 limes
180–200ml coconut milk
100ml maple or brown rice syrup
½ teaspoon turmeric (optional, for colour)
small pinch of salt

For the topping
2 fresh mangoes, thinly sliced

Prepare a 12-hole muffin tin by making a cross in each cup with two long strips of baking paper. This is to help you remove the mini cakes from the tin once they are frozen. The paper needs to stick to the base and sides a little so that it is easy to lift out the cakes. (If you have a silicone muffin tray, you won't need to use paper.)

To make the crust, whizz the desiccated coconut, almonds and dates in a food-processor until they are finely chopped and, when pressed together, a small ball forms. Place 1½ tablespoons of the mixture into each cup of your muffin tray. Firmly press the crust in, either with your fingers or a small glass. Set aside.

To make the filling, heat some water in a pan and add the unopened packet of creamed coconut. Allow to soften before cutting open the packet

and adding the coconut to the bowl of a high-speed blender. Drain the soaked mango and cashew nuts and add to the blender, together with the vanilla powder, lime juice, 180ml of the coconut milk, syrup, turmeric (if using) and salt. Process until very smooth; if you need to add a bit more coconut milk to keep the machine going, add a few tablespoons at a time. Add about 50–60ml (3½ tablespoons) of the mixture to each muffin cup and transfer the tray to the freezer for 2–3 hours.

Remove the tray from the freezer 30 minutes before you wish to serve. Decorate the mini cakes with fresh slices of mango before serving. These mini cakes are a bit like ice cream; they won't hold their shape too long once they are out of the fridge or freezer.

TIP:
These mini cakes can easily be made in advance and kept frozen. Just take them out of the freezer 30 minutes before serving and decorate them just before eating.

OATMEAL AND RAISIN COOKIES

Never had oatmeal? You should! Oatmeal is high in fibre and protein and a source of important vitamins, minerals and antioxidants. Many studies have proven the health benefits of eating oats, including lower blood sugar levels, weight loss and reduced chance of constipation. Oatmeal is often eaten as a porridge in the morning, but it is also a wonderful grain to give texture and bite to baked goods and cookies. This recipe is quick and simple – perfect when you have unexpected visitors for tea or when you fancy a cookie for breakfast instead of porridge.

Makes 8-10

150g wholegrain spelt flour
50g rolled oat flakes
120ml maple syrup
120ml peanut butter (or other nut butter)

70g raisins
¼ teaspoon vanilla powder
pinch of salt

Preheat the oven to 180°C/gas mark 4 and line a baking sheet with baking paper.

Mix all the ingredients in a bowl until combined and knead to make a dough. If the raisins drop out of the mixture, just push them back in.

I like to use measuring cups (¼ cup or ⅓ cup, depending on how large I want my cookies), to get my cookies more or less the same size. Push some of the dough into the measuring cup and take it out to form a ball. Lay your ball on a lined baking sheet and push it down with either a spatula or the back of the measuring cup. On the rim of the cookie some cracks may appear – if you wish, you can make this even with the palm of your (slightly moist) hands. The cookies don't have to look overly pretty, though – they are meant to be a bit rustic. Repeat until all of your dough is used.

Bake the cookies for 15-17 minutes or until golden brown. Remove from the oven and allow to cool on the tray before transferring to a wire rack. To keep them crunchy, store the cookies in a jar with a tight-fitting lid. They will keep for 4-5 days.

APRICOT, CARDAMOM AND PISTACHIO BISCOTTI

There are many different cookies, soft and chewy, crisp and thin, filled or dipped, and almost all of them go well with a cup of tea. A cup of tea is not only an English tradition, but a Dutch one too. In Holland, the first tea and cookie of the day appears at about 10am, and as a child my mum made me a cup of tea after school and served a cookie with it. Perhaps in thousands, maybe millions, of other homes and cultures it is the same. My favourite cookies are the ones for dipping, like the Italian biscotti or cantucci, which, being twice baked, are crunchy and dry – perfect for dipping into a coffee or a glass of vin santo. However, I prefer them dipped in a cup of tea. The crisp Italian-style biscotti in this recipe are intended for just that.

Makes about 30 biscotti

6 tablespoons chilled aquafaba (see page 135)
250g wholegrain spelt flour
1½ teaspoons ground cardamom
½ teaspoon vanilla powder
1 teaspoon baking powder

150g coconut sugar
70ml natural plant-based yogurt
100g raw pistachios, chopped roughly
100g unsulfured dried apricots, chopped into smaller chunks

Preheat the oven to 160°C/gas mark 3 and line a baking tray with baking paper.

Put the aquafaba into a clean bowl and whisk for 4–6 minutes until stiff white peaks form. Sift the flour into another bowl and add the cardamom, vanilla, baking powder and coconut sugar. Add the whipped aquafaba and the yogurt into the dry ingredients and gently mix together. Next add the chopped pistachios and apricots to the dough and mix them in.

Divide the dough in half. With slightly moist hands, form each half into a log about 30cm long and 5cm wide. Carefully transfer each log to the lined baking tray and bake for 30 minutes in the middle of the oven.

When done remove the logs from the oven and leave to cool for 5–7 minutes. Cut the logs into 1–2 cm slices – you will end up with about 30 slices. Lay the slices on your baking sheet and bake for a further 14–16 minutes. Remove the biscotti from the oven and leave them to cool completely for at least 1 hour on a wire rack, so they become really crunchy. These will keep for at least 1 week in an airtight container.

TIP:
These cookies are meant to be dipped into hot herbal tea or a golden milk (see page 170).

BANANA MUFFINS WITH CRUMBLE TOPPING

Sometimes I keep bananas until their skins turn brown and spotty to increase their sweetness. Then I peel the bananas and freeze them for later use in ice cream, banana bread or these spicy muffins with their delicious crunchy topping. Because bananas have natural sweetness, you don't need a lot of additional sweetener. And did you know that one mashed banana can replace one egg in every baked goods recipe? So that is why I am 'going bananas' over brown spotty bananas!

Makes 9

For the crumble topping
2 tablespoons fine oat flakes
1 tablespoon coconut sugar
1 tablespoon almond butter
¼ teaspoon ground cinnamon
pinch of salt

For the batter
300g wholegrain spelt flour
1 teaspoon bicarbonate of soda

1 teaspoon baking powder
1 teaspoon ground cinnamon
½ teaspoon ground ginger (optional)
¼ teaspoon vanilla powder
pinch of salt
3 ripe bananas, mashed
180ml natural plant-based yogurt
120ml maple syrup
50g walnuts, chopped coarsely

Preheat the oven to 180°C/gas mark 4 and line a 9-hole muffin tray with paper cases.

Start by making the crumble topping. Mix all the ingredients with a fork until they form a crumbly texture. Set aside.

To make the muffins, combine the flour, bicarbonate of soda, baking powder, spices and salt in a large bowl. Add the mashed bananas, yogurt and maple syrup to the dry ingredients. Gently mix with a spatula or whisk until all is combined. Now add the walnuts and gently fold them into the batter.

Portion your batter into the muffin cups using an ice cream scoop or a measuring cup to keep your muffins the same size. Top each one with a teaspoon of crumble. Bake the muffins for 20–24 minutes. They are cooked if a wooden skewer inserted into the muffin comes out clean; if there are some crumbs or there is moist dough clinging to it, then cook them for a few minutes longer. When done, take the muffins out of the oven and leave to cool.

These are best eaten within 4–5 days.

PLUM GALETTE

During a good plum year I eat and make lots of plum dishes. In the area where we live in France, there are just so many varieties. First the purple 'Madeleine' will be ripe, then the small yellow 'Mirabelle' and, in late August, the 'Quetsche' or damson. If there are plenty, it means I have buckets full. They will be eaten as a snack or in a tart. Some women in the village will preserve them in glass jars, to make plum cakes all year round. I prefer freezing them or even better, eating them straight away in an easy galette-style tart like this one.

Serves 6-8

For the dough
160g wholegrain spelt flour
100g almond butter
pinch of salt
1½ tablespoons coconut blossom sugar or maple syrup
6-7 tablespoons ice-cold water

For the filling
500g plums, halved, stoned and sliced
2-3 tablespoons coconut blossom sugar or maple syrup

¼ teaspoon vanilla powder
a few turns of black pepper (optional, but really good)
1 teaspoon cornflour, arrowroot or tapioca flour

For the glaze (optional)
2 tablespoons almond milk (or other plant-based milk)
1 tablespoon maple syrup
2-3 tablespoons coconut blossom sugar

To make the dough, put all the ingredients except the water into a food-processor. Pulse to form a dough and add the cold water tablespoon by tablespoon. When all the water is incorporated, the dough should still be a bit crumbly but, when pushed together, it should hold. Tip the dough out of the bowl and form a ball, wrap it in clingfilm and leave to chill in the fridge for about 30 minutes (or put into the freezer for 10 minutes if you are in a hurry).

Preheat the oven to 180°C/gas mark 4 and line a baking tray with baking paper.

Make the filling by gently combining the plums, sugar or syrup, vanilla powder, black pepper (if using) and cornflour in a bowl. Set aside.

Remove the dough from the fridge and roll it out with a lightly floured rolling pin on a clean, lightly floured surface. (If it is hard to roll, leave the dough for a few minutes at room temperature to soften slightly.) Form into a circle about 30-35cm diameter and 0.5cm thick. Transfer the flat dough to the lined baking tray. Place the plum mixture in the centre of the dough, or fan it out to make the filling look prettier, leaving a 4-5cm border. Fold in the border over the filling. Now, whisk the almond milk and the maple syrup in a small bowl and brush it over the dough border, followed by a sprinkle of coconut blossom sugar.

Bake for 40-50 minutes or until the pastry is golden brown and the plums are cooked. Leave to cool. Serve as is or with a dollop of Cashew Soured Cream (see page 17) or coconut yogurt.

ORANGE AND ROSEMARY TARTELETTES

Serving individual cakes must be the fanciest thing around and when I make them I almost feel like a real French pâtissier. If you don't usually have the patience to bake individual cakes, these tartelettes are easy to make. Try to use blood oranges for the filling, they are so pretty and taste sweeter than regular oranges. You will need six individual tart tins, preferably ones with removable bases.

Makes 6

For the crust
2 tablespoons ground (golden) flaxseeds
100g oat flour, plus extra for dusting
125g blanched almond flour
3 tablespoons maple syrup
3 tablespoons nut butter (white almond or
   cashew if you want to keep the tartelettes pale)
pinch of salt

For the cream filling
200g raw cashews, soaked for at least
   30 minutes

180ml fresh orange juice
1½ teaspoons orange zest
½ teaspoon vanilla powder
1 teaspoon freshly grated ginger (optional)
2–3 tablespoons maple or brown rice syrup

To decorate
3 (blood) oranges, peeled and segmented
1 teaspoon fresh rosemary leaves, finely
   chopped

Start by preparing the crust for the tartelettes. Combine the ground flaxseeds with 6 tablespoons (90ml) of water and stir well. Set aside to allow the mixture to thicken; this will be your flaxseed 'egg'.

In another large bowl use a fork to combine the oat flour, almond flour, maple syrup, nut butter, flaxseed mix and salt. When the dough comes together, form it into a ball. Cover the bowl with a plate and put in the fridge for 20–30 minutes.

Preheat the oven to 180°C/gas mark 4 while you make the filling. Combine all the ingredients in a high-speed blender, and mix until very smooth. Transfer the filling to a container and put in the fridge.

Remove the dough from the fridge and roll it out thinly, using a little more oat flour if it is sticking to the surface. Use a cutter to stamp out rounds about 3cm bigger than the tart tins. Drape the dough into the six tins, gently pushing it into the bases and sides, and cut off any excess dough. Bake in the oven for 20–25 minutes until golden brown. Remove from the oven and allow to cool enough to handle. Gently remove the tins.

Distribute the orange cream filling over the crusts and decorate with orange segments and a small sprinkle of finely chopped fresh rosemary. Serve immediately or keep in the fridge until ready to serve.

STRAWBERRY AND VANILLA CUSTARD TART

I think it's good to wait for the local strawberry season. Sure, we can get strawberries, and almost any other fruit, all year round, but it just isn't the same. The global market has meant that we've lost touch with seasonality over the last few decades. In an age when everything seems possible, sometimes it is better to step back and start thinking about how things were done in the old days. Eagerly awaiting the season for a certain fruit or vegetable is one example. So, when local strawberries are available this recipe is highly recommended.

Serves 6–8

For the crust
200g almond flour
3 tablespoons arrowroot or cornflour
4 tablespoons coconut sugar
80ml natural plant-based yogurt
pinch of salt

For the custard
450ml almond milk (for a homemade version see page 98)

¾ teaspoon vanilla powder
pinch of salt
4–5 tablespoons maple or brown rice syrup
pinch of turmeric (optional, for colour)
1 teaspoon agar agar
3 tablespoons cornflour or arrowroot
750g strawberries, halved

Preheat the oven to 180°C/gas mark 4 and line the removable base of a 20cm tart tin with baking paper.

Using a fork, combine the ingredients for the crust in a large bowl until a dough forms. Press it into the tart tin with moist hands or the back of a spoon. (The dough is quite soft, so you might have to rewet your hands from time to time.) Make a layer on the base and then press it to the sides, ensuring the crust is evenly distributed.

Place the crust in the oven for about 20–30 minutes until it is golden brown. Remove the crust from the oven and let it cool enough to handle, then gently remove the crust from the tin.

While your tart bakes, you can make the custard filling. Gently bring the almond milk to the boil,

add the vanilla powder, salt, sweetener, turmeric (if using) and agar agar. Stir continuously with a whisk until the agar agar dissolves and there are no small lumps. Cook for 6 minutes, whisking frequently. Taste to check that it is sweet enough to your liking.

Combine the cornflour or arrowroot with 2 tablespoons of water and add this to the gently boiling custard. Whisk briskly to thicken the custard. After 1 minute, remove the custard from the heat and leave to cool a little.

Once the tart crust is cool, pour in the vanilla custard. Leave to cool and set completely – you can transfer the tart to the fridge to speed up the process. Once the custard is set and cooled, top with strawberries and serve.

RAW BROWNIE PETIT FOURS

When friends come over or I am invited for a meal, one of the things I often make is a treat that contains no refined sugar. A lot of people have their own ideas about being vegan and sugar-free, most of which are not very positive. But if they taste one of my vegan and sugar-free cookies or tarts, they are swept off their feet and ask me all sorts of questions. What did I use? How come they've never had this before? Is it really healthy? These pretty brownies will certainly impress your guests.

Makes about 30 pieces
For the base
300g Medjool dates, stoned
150g desiccated coconut
150g raw walnuts
pinch of salt
½ teaspoon vanilla powder
4 tablespoons cacao or carob powder

For the cream layer
100g creamed coconut (or coconut butter)
200g raw cashews, soaked overnight and drained

½ teaspoon vanilla powder
80ml maple syrup or brown rice syrup
160-180ml coconut or almond milk
pinch of salt

Topping suggestions
freeze-dried raspberries or strawberries, fresh berries or fruits, sesame seeds, chopped raw pistachios or cacao nibs, orange or lemon zest and edible flowers

---

Line the base of a brownie tin with baking paper.

Pulse the ingredients for the base in a food processor until an even texture forms, scraping down the sides from time to time.

Press the mixture into the lined brownie tin (or into some silicon ice-cube trays, in which case leave some space for the second layer).

Now make the cream layer. Bring some water to a simmer in a small pan and place the creamed coconut, in its original packaging (either plastic or a glass jar), into the water until it becomes liquid. Measure off 100g into the bowl of a high-speed blender.

Add the soaked, drained cashews to the liquid creamed coconut, together with the vanilla, maple syrup, 160ml of the nut milk and salt.

Blend until very smooth. If necessary add up to 20ml extra milk to ensure the mixture continues to blend, scraping down the sides if needed. Once smooth, spread this mixture over the base layer in your brownie tin or in the silicon trays. Chill for at least 30 minutes.

When chilled, turn out the brownie from the tin and cut into 30 squares to make the petit fours, or, if you used ice cube trays, simply turn out the petit fours from the moulds. Place them on a plate or lined tray, allowing a little space between them. Return the petit fours to the freezer for 2-3 hours. Bring the petit fours to room temperature 20-30 minutes before you want to serve them, and decorate with a topping of your choice.

These petit fours can also be left frozen. They will keep for 3 months in the freezer.

SPONGE CAKE WITH BLACKBERRY JAM AND THYME

Wild blackberries can grow almost everywhere. When I was younger you could find them on abandoned pieces of land, in hedgerows, along roadsides and railtracks, etc. But they seem to be less common these days. Wasteland has been used and people's gardens are cleaned up, so there isn't much unclaimed space left for the blackberry. It's a shame, because we need these pieces of land to preserve the wild plants and the insects that live on it. So, maintain your garden a little less and you will have more time to make this delicious jam to layer into a sponge cake. The jam is made with little sweetener and thickened with chia seeds, so there is no need for lengthy boiling.

Serves 8

For the cake
125g wholegrain flour
2 teaspoons baking powder
½ teaspoon vanilla powder
pinch of salt
125g coconut blossom sugar
125g natural plant-based yogurt
9 tablespoons (120ml) chilled aquafaba (see page 135), whisked into stiff white peaks

For the jam
250g blackberries (defrosted if frozen)
160ml water or apple juice
1 tablespoon lemon juice
2–3 tablespoons maple or brown rice syrup
½ teaspoon vanilla powder
1 teaspoon fresh thyme leaves
4 tablespoons chia seeds

To decorate
125g blackberries
fresh thyme leaves

Preheat the oven to 180°C/gas mark 4 and line the base of two 20cm springform cake tins with baking paper.

To make the cake, combine all the dry ingredients in a bowl. Using a spatula, gently fold in the yogurt and aquafaba until evenly mixed.

Divide the batter evenly between the cake tins. Bake for 20–25 minutes until a cocktail stick inserted into the centre comes out clean.

Meanwhile, make the blackberry jam. Put the blackberries, water or apple juice, lemon juice, sweetener, vanilla and thyme into a pan over a low heat and bring gently to the boil. Stir frequently to prevent it sticking. When the water is bubbling, cook for 3–4 minutes and then mash the blackberries down with a fork. Remove from the heat and stir in the chia seeds. It takes about 10 minutes to thicken. Set aside. This step can also be done in advance.

When the cakes are cooked, remove them from the oven. Allow to cool in the tins a little then turn out onto wire racks and peel away the baking paper. Once they have cooled, spread half the blackberry jam over one cake and place the other cake on top. Spread with the remaining jam and dot with fresh blackberries and thyme leaves.

LEMON AND BLUEBERRY POLENTA CAKE

After a 40-minute drive from my French home, following roads that get smaller and smaller, I finally arrive at a spot where, in mid-summer, you can pick your own blueberries. Nowhere will you see advertisements for this spot; people just seem to know. You see them walking back to their cars laden with kilos of blueberries for the year to come. I normally pick about 8 kilos of blueberries, but they never last more than a month. Blueberries eaten straight, blueberry and banana ice cream, blueberry dressing (see page 21) and this blueberry cake. Blueberries and lemon are a match made in heaven and this polenta cake is beautifully light, thanks to the aquafaba.

Serves 6–8

6 tablespoons (90 ml) aquafaba (see page 135),
  chilled for at least 6 hours
130g fine polenta
75g almond flour
¾ teaspoon baking powder
¾ teaspoon bicarbonate of soda

120ml maple syrup
80ml natural plant-based yogurt
zest and juice of 1½ lemons
300g blueberries (or substitute with blackberries
  or, in winter, orange slices)

Preheat the oven to 180°C/gas mark 4 and line the base of a 22cm springform cake tin with baking paper.

Pour the aquafaba into the bowl of a stand mixer (or use a hand-held mixer) and whisk until stiff white peaks form. It will take about 4–6 minutes.

Mix all the dry ingredients in a separate bowl and set aside.

Gently fold the yogurt, maple syrup, lemon zest and juice into the aquafaba with a spatula. Then carefully mix this into the dry ingredients by folding it in, again with a spatula. When mixed, stir 200g of the blueberries into the batter.

Scrape the batter into the cake tin and gently press the remaining 100g blueberries on top.

Cook for about 40 minutes. You can check the cake is done by inserting a wooden skewer into the centre. If it comes out clean the cake is cooked; if not, it needs a minute or two longer. Remove the cake from the oven and leave to cool a little in the tin then turn out onto a wire rack to cool completely. Serve with a dollop of coconut yogurt or Cashew Soured Cream (see page 17) and extra fresh berries.

APPLE CINNAMON CAKE WITH CHAI DRIZZLE

The smell of a warm apple tart with cinnamon just instantly brings me back to my childhood at my grandparents' house. On autumn weekends my grandfather would make a tart using the apples from his allotment which he so carefully maintained. I watched him making the cake and although this vegan version is completely different, I know he will like it.

Serves 8–10

For the cake
6 tablespoons (90ml) chilled aquafaba (see page 135)
250g wholegrain spelt flour (or use gluten-free flour)
1½ teaspoons baking powder
1½ teaspoons bicarbonate of soda
2½ teaspoons ground cinnamon
175g coconut sugar
pinch of salt
180ml natural plant-based yogurt
2 medium apples, coarsely grated

for the chai drizzle
5 tablespoons raw white cashew butter (or white almond butter)
60ml maple syrup
1 teaspoon vanilla powder
1½ teaspoons ground cinnamon
½ teaspoon freshly grated nutmeg
seeds from 1 cardamom pod
small pinch of black pepper
1½ teaspoons freshly grated ginger
pinch of salt

Preheat the oven to 180°C/gas mark 4. Line the base of a 20cm springform tin with baking paper.

Whisk the aquafaba in a clean bowl until stiff white peaks form. Set aside.

Sift the flour into a separate bowl and add the baking powder, bicarbonate of soda, cinnamon, coconut sugar and salt. Mix the ingredients and gently mix in the yogurt, whipped aquafaba and grated apple. Transfer this mixture to the cake tin. Bake for 50–60 minutes. Check if it is ready by inserting a skewer into the centre of the cake. If it comes out clean, the cake is done; if any mixture clings to the skewer, cook the cake for an additional 5 minutes and try again.

Remove the cake from the oven and allow to cool a little in the tin before turning out and transferring to a wire rack to cool completely.

Meanwhile, make your drizzle by mixing all the ingredients in a blender. You may need to add a little nut milk, a tablespoon at a time, to thin. Be careful though: the more liquid you add, the runnier your drizzle will become. Once the cake has cooled completely, pour over the chai drizzle.

CINNAMON AND RAISIN BREAD WITH ALMOND MARZIPAN

Stol is a sweet Dutch bread filled with raisins that has an almond paste in the centre. It is eaten at Christmas time and at Easter. Other European countries have similar breads, such as pannetone in Italy and *osterbrot* in Germany. The one thing typically Dutch is the almond paste in the middle of the *stol*. This almond paste or marzipan often contains egg, or sometimes cream: not very vegan. So I wanted to make my own version of this bread. It's a nice breakfast bread (with some nut butter) or it can be served at tea time.

Makes one loaf/10-12 slices

150g raisins
150ml apple juice
1 teaspoon dried yeast
3 tablespoons coconut sugar
180ml plant-based milk
1 tablespoon ground flaxseeds
325g wholegrain spelt flour
2 teaspoons ground cinnamon

for the almond paste
100g blanched almond flour
5 Medjool dates, stoned
60ml apple juice

Start by soaking the raisins in a small bowl with the apple juice.

In another small bowl, combine the yeast, coconut sugar and 40ml of the plant milk. Stir well and set aside for about 5 minutes. The mixture may begin to fizz a bit, but if it doesn't that's fine. This yeast mixture is a good start for your bread to leaven.

In a third bowl combine the flaxseeds with 3 tablespoons of water. Set aside for 5 minutes so you will get a flaxseed 'egg'.

Combine the flour, yeast, flaxseed 'egg', cinnamon and the remaining plant milk in a large bowl. Start to knead the mixture. If the mixture feels a bit too dry, add a little more milk or water. If it is too wet and keeps sticking to your hands, add in a little flour but not too much; often the dough will improve after a couple of minutes of

kneading and too much flour will result in a very dense bread.

After kneading the dough for a couple of minutes in the bowl, you can tip it onto a lightly floured surface and knead for a further 8-10 minutes. Transfer your dough back to your bowl and cover with a clean towel. Leave to rise for 2-3 hours in a warm space until doubled in volume (you can also do this the night before you want to bake your bread).

Make the almond paste by blending the blanched almond flour with the dates and apple juice – you can use a small blender or food processor for this – until a smooth paste forms. Roll the paste into a log shape about 25cm long, wrap in baking paper or clingfilm and let it rest in the fridge for at least 30 minutes. The taste will improve with time, so this too can be made the night before.

When the dough has doubled in volume you can continue making your bread. Drain the raisins and work them into the dough. Form a log on a floured surface and flatten this a bit, then place your almond paste in the middle of the dough. Fold the sides of the dough over the almond paste and turn over the entire bread so the folds are underneath. Now leave to rise for a further 30 minutes.

Preheat the oven to 180°C/gas mark 4 and line a baking tray with baking paper. Once the dough has risen for 30 minutes transfer it to the lined tray and cook for about 40–50 minutes. The bread should look golden brown and if you tap the underside it should sound hollow. Remove the bread from the oven and leave to cool before slicing and eating.

TIP:

Make this bread truly festive by choosing from the following options to make it your own: swap the raisins for chopped apricots, sugar-free dried cranberries or chopped up dates; enhance the flavour by adding two teaspoons of organic orange zest; add a handful of your favourite chopped nuts; or swap one teaspoon of the ground cinnamon for ground cardamom. To decorate, you could sift coconut flour or ground xylitol (birch sugar) over the top for a snowy finish.

GOLDEN TURMERIC MILK

This warming, aromatic and sweet drink is coloured and flavoured with turmeric and other spices. Golden milk, also known as *Haldi doodh* in Hindi, has its origin in Ayurveda (the Indian traditional medicine system). It is now very popular and served in healthy juice bars and cafés all over the world. I prefer to drink it at a friend's place because she makes an incredibly delicious version. Her secret is to add Medjool dates and leave the milk to simmer for a long time. This recipe is inspired by her turmeric milk.

Serves 2–3

750ml plant-based or nut milk of choice
thumb-sized piece of fresh ginger, peeled
  and sliced
thumb-sized piece of fresh sliced turmeric, or
  2 teaspoons powdered turmeric
1 cinnamon stick

5 cardamom pods, lightly bruised
pinch of black pepper
1 star anise (optional)
1 teaspoon lemon or orange zest
½ teaspoon vanilla powder
2 Medjool dates, stoned

Put all the ingredients into a pan and bring gently to the boil over a low heat. Once it comes to the boil, turn down and leave to simmer for about 20–30 minutes. Strain the milk through a sieve and pour it into a blender, adding the Medjool dates left in the sieve. Whizz up until frothy and serve.

TIP:
This milk can be drunk hot or cold, or mixed with chia seeds to make a golden chia pudding.

INDEX

ACKNOWLEDGEMENTS

Thank you to dear Dick and Olivia for your support and the love you give me everyday. I am grateful for the warmth and love I have received from my parents, who planted the seed for my healthy food passion. I am thankful and humble for the support and guidance I get from Jos and Saskia regarding food and health. Big thanks to my sweet friends Anne, Armijn, Albert, Suzanne, Alja and Robert, who always believed in and supported my culinary work. Brecht, for making me treats when I am tired and just for being such a dear friend. Thank you Suzanne and Tamara for inspiring food get togethers and for your positivity. I'd like to thank all of my family and friends for their positivity and kindness.

Thanks to the people that bought my first book *Vegan in 7* for their support. It means the world to me knowing that so many people are cooking plant-based food and are positively contributing to their health, the health of others and our planet. I am grateful for my many followers on Instagram (@ritaserano) for the positivity and kindness I receive. Without them, there wouldn't be a book in the first place. Social media, if used wisely and independently, can be such a wonderful platform for making connections with people all around the world. Here people can contribute to each others' dreams, learnings and teachings on different levels and from different cultures. Their support inspires me every day to create delicious and healthy plant-based recipes.

Thank you to Kyle Books and the whole team for making this book come alive and making my food dreams come true. I especially would like to thank Judith Hannam, my editor Tara O'Sullivan and her assistant Sarah Kyle for making me a part of the whole book creating process. Clare Winfield for the gorgeous photography, Joss Herd and India for the beautiful food styling, Linda Berlin for getting me gorgeous props and Georgia Vaux for designing this book. Furthermore I would like to thank copy editor Stephanie Evans and the production team Nic Jones, Gemma John and Emily Noto.

And without any doubt I would like to thank you all, who are now reading these lines. Grab my hand and use this book to be Vegan for Good!